MUKUNDA DEB

MUKUNDA DEB
Godabarish Mishra

Translated by
Bhagabat Nath

BLACK EAGLE BOOKS
Dublin, USA | Bhubaneswar, India

Black Eagle Books
USA address:
7464 Wisdom Lane
Dublin, OH 43016

India address:
E/312, Trident Galaxy, Kalinga Nagar,
Bhubaneswar-751003, Odisha, India

E-mail: info@blackeaglebooks.org
Website: www.blackeaglebooks.org

First International Edition Published by
Black Eagle Books, 2025

MUKUNDA DEB
by Godabarish Mishra

Translated by Bhagabat Nath

Original Copyright © **Godabarish Mishra**
Translation Copyright © **Bhagabat Nath**

All rights reserved. No part of this publication may be reproduced, stored in a retrieval system, or transmitted, in any form or by any means, electronic, mechanical, photocopying, recording or otherwise without the prior permission of the publisher.

Cover & Interior Design: Ezy's Publication

ISBN- 978-1-64560-801-1 (Paperback)

Printed in the United States of America

Introduction

Pandit Godabarish Mishra (26 October 1886 – 26 July 1956) is a versatile genius and prolific writer. He has contributed significantly to Odia literature. He was a teacher, litterateur, social reformer, editor, legislator, minister, and an architect of modern Odisha. He played a stellar role in the establishment of Utkal University, the Odisha High court and various colleges in Puri, Baleshwar and Sambalpur districts and conversion of medical school of Cuttack into a medical college. He was a poet, novelist, playwright, short story writer and a biographer. As a poet he enormously used the lyric and the ballad.

His poetry is based on history and legends and a complete reflection of his romantic persona in the opinion of Dr. Mayadhar Mansingh. His *Alekhika* (1923) is a collection of his ten magnificent ballads that includes his famous ballad "Kalijai". His collection of poems like *Chayanika, Kalika* (1921), *Kishalaya* (1922), *Geetayana* and *Geetiguchha* (1957) are treasure troves of lyric poetry. His lyrics depict nationalism, social awareness, beauty of rural life and empathy for human beings. He has authored four novels: *Ghatantar, Abhagini, Athar Saha Satar* and *Nirbasit. Abhagini* deals with the conflicts of Banki and Khordha with the British during 1840. *Athar Saha Satar* (1817) delineates the

Paika Mutiny of Khordha and the dedication of the glorious patriot, Buxi Jagabandhu.

His oeuvre is enriched by two historical plays: *Purushottam Deb* (1917) and *Mukunda Deb* (1920). These plays are vibrant with history, humanity and patriotism. He has written these to historical plays to make the people of Odisha during the British rule aware of their glorious past and inspire them with patriotic emotions.

The play *Mukunda Deb* is based on the historical facts contained in the Madalapanji, the official chronicle of the Temple of Lord Jagannath. Mishra was also aware of the *History of Odisha* by Sir William Hunter and again by Andrew Stirling, the *History of Odisha* by Pyari Mohan Acharya. He has faithfully maintained the historical figures like Badshah Akbar; Suleman Karrani, the ruler of Banga, Kalapahad, his son-in-law and General of Banga Army; and Hassan Khan, a general of Badshah Akbar. besides Mukunda Deb, the last independent Hindu king of Odisha and perfidious Ramachandra Bhanja, the king of Saranga Garh and an aspirant of the throne of Odisha. He has carefully represented the characters like Shikhi, Manai and Dhurjati who are the loyal followers of Ramachandra Bhanja to bring out the best villainous intent in them. These three are the most heinous characters in history. Mishra has introduced a few characters who are the products of his imagination so as to make the play appealing to the audience.

The playwright has roped in several legends and folk tales to add authenticity to the historical events. One such tale is about the structure of *Kahali*, a musical instrument played in temples and religious ceremonies. While returning after his successful expedition to Banga, Mukunda Deb sits in meditation on the bank of Ganga. He has strict orders that he should not be disturbed until his meditation is over. He has commanded that he who disturbs his meditation shall be cut into three pieces. The clever Minister utilises the services of a Kahalia to raise Mukunda Deb from his meditation by playing on his *Kahali*. It is explained to the irate King that it is only a *Kahali* that has disturbed him. Consequently, *Kahali* which was a single piece of musical instrument till then is cut into three pieces. Since then, *Kahali* is made up of three pieces. The playwright makes use of this folk tale in his play.

The plot of the play revolves around the glorious achievements and ignominious death of Mukunda Deb. The throne of Utkal is vacant after the premature demise of King Raghurama who has died just one year after the death of King Narasingha. The Minister and the Army Chief along with some citizens plead with Mukunda Deb to be the king. He is initially reluctant. Moreover, King Ramachandra Bhanja, the ruler of Saranga Garh is eager to be the king. Mukunda Deb writes a letter to Ramachandra Bhanja inviting him to adorn the throne of Utkal. But he spurns the offer. Mukunda Deb hesitantly accepts the offer as his duty to Mother Utkal and Lord Jagannath.

Ramachandra Bhanja urges his servant Dhurjati to assassinate Mukunda Deb as he has already proved his talent as an assassin secretly killing Narasingha and Raghurama Chhotray. Dhurjati is unwilling to murder Mukunda Deb as he is the most suitable claimant to the throne and he feels diffident to put out the only shining star in the political firmament of Utkal.

In the meantime, Badshah Akbar seeks the help of Mukunda Deb to put down the rebellion of Nawab Suleman, the ruler of Banga. Hasan Khan, a General of Badshah Akbar approaches Mukunda Deb to negotiate with the Gajapati king. Mukunda Deb acquiesces to help in spite of opposition from the Minister and the Chief of Utkal Army. Only the old General Dhanurdhar Baliarsingh supports his king. Baliarsingh inspires ten thousand villagers with patriotism and they come forward to fight along with their king. The Minister and the Army Chief make arrangements for the protection of Barabati Fort. Barabati is to be protected by Koni Samant Singhar having ten thousand soldiers with him and Purandar Jagadeb is to assist him with ten thousand soldiers. The Minister and the Army Chief are to proceed to the border with fifty thousand soldiers to reinforce the strength of their king.

Kalapahad, the General of Banga Army meets Mukunda Deb on the battle front. He suggests to Mukunda Deb to support the Nawab of Banga and desist from fighting. Mukunda Deb refuses on the ground that he would not betray Badshah Akbar who reposes faith in him as a friend. Kalapahad returns with a warning to the King to be ready to face Afghan wrath in the battle field. In battle that followed between Mukunda Deb and Suleman, the Nawab of Banga, the Nawab is defeated and injured. Mukunda Deb is gracious enough to stop war and attends on the Nawab. The Nawab is surprised by Mukunda Deb's generous gesture and is overwhelmed by his hospitality. Kalapahad is defeated and taken as a prisoner. When he is brought to the presence of Mukunda Deb, the magnanimous King of Odisha sets him free instead of punishing him. At this point, the Minister and the Army Chief enter and crown Mukunda Deb king.

In the meantime, Shikhi and Manai, two vassals of Ramachandra Bhanja of Saranga Garh, approach Kalapahad for his help. They offer him the entire northern territory from the banks of Ganga to the Subarnarekha to win his support for Ramachandra Bhanja while the southern territory from the Subarnarekha to the Godavari will be retained by Bhanja. They will guide Kalapahad and his army through a very secret path; through the dense forest and hills in the absence of Mukunda Deb, the Minister and the Army Chief from the capital. Kalapahad greedily accepts the offer and in due course is ready to lay siege on the Barabati Fort. When Queen Ushayinee receives the message that Kalapahad is approaching Barabati to demolish it, she is ready to encounter Kalapahad and issues necessary orders to Koni Samantasinghar, the Commandant of Barabati Fort, to be on the alert. In the meantime, she receives a letter from Leelabati, her childhood friend and the queen of Ramachandra Bhanja requesting her for military support to encounter Kalapahad. She despatches a troop of ten thousand soldiers to her.

In the battle field on the bank of Ganga, the Nawab is distressed to receive the message that Kalapahad is wreaking havoc in Odisha by demolishing Hindu deities and temples in the villages and cities. He proceeds to the camp of Mukunda Deb when Shikhi and Manai in disguise are attempting to murder the king. He kills both of them and saves Mukunda Deb.

Mukunda Deb returns to Odisha and wins several battles against Ramachandra Bhanja on his way to his capital at Cuttack. The king of Saranga Garh reaches Mukunda Deb's camp with a flag of truce. While Mukunda Deb was reflecting on the proposal of peace, Ramachandra Bhanja takes out a secret weapon from his attire, attacks Mukunda Deb and inflicts mortal wounds on him. Mukunda Deb collapses and Bhanja escapes. Mukunda Deb passes away in the presence of the Minister and the Army Chief.

It is a historical fact that Mukunda Deb on his return

from Banga he confronts Ramachandra Bhanja with a large army. In the battle at Gohiratikiri, a place near modern Jajpur, Mukunda Deb was killed during the war. But the playwright creates a myth on the death of his hero to glorify him as a tragic hero. He presents Ramachandra Bhanja as an assassin to secretly murder Mukunda Deb while offering him the proposal for peace. This deviation is a dramatic innovation to depict Ramachandra Bhanja as a heinous character and garner sympathy for his hero, Mukunda Deb.

Ramachandra Bhanja negotiates with the Minister, the Army Chief and Dhanurdhar Baliarsingh to fight Kalapahad. They agree to help but they are not willing to leave Barabati Fort to him. Kalapahad is summoned by the Nawab to return to his kingdom. But he imprisons Dillir Khan, the ambassador of the Nawab. Kalapahad is determined to enter Barabati Fort. In a meeting with Ramachandra Bhanja, Kalapahad imprisons him. Ramachandra Bhanja loses his mind and becomes a mental wreck. His Queen Leelabati pleads with Kalapahad and makes him free. Kalapahad defeats the army of Utkal and lays siege on the Fort. Queen Ushayinee, her daughter Chitrotpala and the women of the city enter the funeral pyre and immolate themselves.

History is silent on the names of the queens of Ramachandra Bhanja and Mukunda Deb. But the playwright has introduced Leelabati as the queen of Ramachandra Bhanja and Ushayinee as the queen of Mukunda Deb and Chitrotpala as their daughter for dramatic necessity. He perhaps feels that the audience may not appreciate a play without female protagonists.

The playwright has given his best efforts to portray Mukunda Deb as a heroic, generous and magnanimous hero. His meeting with Suleman, the Nawab of Banga, and Kalapahad, the Army Commandant of Banga highlight his magnanimity. He has been depicted as a tragic hero. The female characters and the supporting characters have been given adequate attention to enhance the dramatic appeal. The dialogues mostly generate heroic sentiments but humours created by minor characters are appropriate. There are songs sung by queens, maids, soldiers, and minor characters that show prevailing dramatic tradition. The playwright has written these plays not only to entertain his audience but also to educate them with the glorious history of Odisha.

However, there are certain scenes which cannot be performed on stage. For example, the city women entering the funeral pyre one by one to immolate themselves is nearly impossible to perform on stage and is outrageous for the audience. They should have been narrated on stage by either Queen Ushayinee or any other character while the action should have been performed off stage by means of stage craft. Queen Ushayinee kicking Kalapahad in the final scene seems incongruous. The playwright intends to conclude his play with humiliating Kalapahad perhaps please his audience. In spite of these incongruities the play has been rated as an outstanding tragedy and Godabarish Mishra stands out as a unique playwright.

- Bhagabat Nath

CAST

Male
Mukunda Deb
Minister of Odisha
Chief of the Army
Dhanurdhar Baliarsingh : A Feudal Chief
Ramachandra Bhanja : King of Sarang Garh
Minister of Sarang Garh
Sadasib and Raghunath : The Courtiers of Sarang Garh
Shikhi and Manai : Messengers of
  Ramachandra Bhanja
Banambar : A citizen of Sarang Garh
Dhurjati : a servant of Ramachandra Bhanja
Suleman Shah : Nawab of Banga
Kalapahad : The General of Banga Army
Dillir Khan : A courtier of Banga
Hasan Khan : A messenger of Akbar
Gobind and Gopal : citizens of Odisha
Narayan : Guard
Other Guards, soldiers, pipers and citizens

Female
Ushayinee : The Queen of Mukunda Deb
Chitrotpala : The daughter of Mukunda Deb
Leelabati : The Queen of
  Ramachandra Bhanja
Ladies, hand maids, attendants, dancers etc.

ACT I

SCENE I
The Chamber of Mukunda Deb.

(*Mukunda Deb, Minister of Odisha, Chief of Odisha Army, and citizens are seated.*)

MUKUNDA : Why this proposal again, esteemed Minister? I'll continue to rule the kingdom as I am doing now. What is the need of adorning the throne? I have told it to you several times. Why do you keep quiet? Well, first of all I'm not a contender to the throne. I'm an humble citizen. Since the kingdom was in uncertainty without a suitable king, administration of the kingdom was vested with me. Therefore, I am not the king nor am I the most suitable candidate for kingship.

CHIEF : Will the state be without a king?

MUKUNDA : I too don't wish that. Please, nominate somebody who is suitable for the throne. I shall serve him as a servant. I am not a leader but a servant of Mother Utkal.

MINISTER : We have nominated you as our leader. You are the most suitable candidate for the throne.

CHIEF : The citizens too have selected you.

CITIZENS : We, the people of all the cities and villages, have unanimously selected you. You have to accept our prayer.

CHIEF	:	It is not the prayer of the citizens but the prayer of the state, the prayer of the motherland before her choicest son.
MINISTER	:	You may ignore the prayer of Mother Utkal, if you so like.
MUKUNDA	:	Well, Mr. Minister, you may leave now. I shall send you the message later.
CHIEF	:	What message? We don't want any message other than your consent. You can give it to us now.
MUKUNDA	:	No, please wait. For some time. However, Mr. Minister, I have told you earlier. Why are you silent now?
MINISTER	:	You'll give your consent later. What do you mean by 'later'? Before evening.
MUKUNDA	:	No, not 'consent'. It's 'message'. There are differences between these two, Mr. Minister.
MINISTER	:	What is 'message' for you is 'consent' for us.
MUKUNDA	:	How marvellous your language is! Please wait, I shall let you know.
MINISTER	:	Please tell that you agree. Let's take your leave.
CITIZENS	:	It's not only our prayer but also of the people of the entire kingdom. You have to fulfill our prayer.
		(*All but Mukunda exit.*)
MUKUNDA	:	The ruler of this vast kingdom of Utkal! I came here just as a servant. The kingdom was without a king. I have achieved this high position by dint of good governance. It can be said that I am the *de facto* ruler.

What more? I have so far been standing beneath the throne of the king, carrying out his commands and performing my duties. How I can be seated on this gem-studded throne of Mother Utkal and give commands to others! No, it is a great sin. What else was Gobinda Bidyadhar? Of course, the kingdom is without a king. Firstly, it is devastated. Secondly, valiant Mughals and Muslims are at large. Can the state remain vulnerable at this hour? No, a suitable leader is required. Is it me? How can I be? My heart is blowing up at the plight of the kingdom. Mother Utkal, lead kindly light; urge my conscience; convey my duties to me. Oh, Lord Jagannath! You are guiding the whole universe from your seat at Neelachal. Show me the right path at this hour of misfortune. On one hand there is my kingdom, on the other hand there is my lack of personal interest. (*Ushayinee enters.*)
Who is there? Ushayinee?

USHA : Why do you look so worried? Death is inevitable in the world. Someone dies first and someone else dies later.
MUKUNDA : It's, of course, true, Ushayinee.
USHA : Then, why are you so sad?
MUKUNDA : I am unhappy for the kingdom, Ushayinee, not for any individual. King Raghurama had to die, whether tomorrow or today. Similarly, King Narasingha died a year ago.

USHA	:	Then, death is a regular affair with this kingship.
MUKUNDA	:	Yes, of course.
USHA	:	King Raghurama died just one year after the death of King Narasingha.
MUKUNDA	:	Before one scar is healed, the Lord cuts a new scar in the heart of the subjects.
USHA	:	How can sorrow help now? Now the governance of the kingdom is entrusted with you. You are almost the king till another king adorns the throne.
MUKUNDA	:	That is the most critical problem, Ushayinee.
USHA	:	What?
MUKUNDA	:	People say that there will be no other king in the state.
USHA	:	What were they telling? Who? When?
MUKUNDA	:	They were telling it long since. You are, of course, not aware of it.
USHA	:	What were they telling?
MUKUNDA	:	There will be no other king in the state.
USHA	:	Will the status quo be maintained? Sheer anarchy?
MUKUNDA	:	No.
USHA	:	Then.
MUKUNDA	:	They are telling – of course, they have taken amiss –
USHA	:	What?
MUKUNDA	:	They are telling me to be the king.
USHA	:	No? What did you tell?
MUKUNDA	:	I agreed.
USHA	:	No?
MUKUNDA	:	What else should I tell?

USHA	:	No. You might have refused.
MUKUNDA	:	Of course, I refused. I have, in one way, said "Yes", Ushayinee. However, in their absence. The anxiety you have marked in me while you came in is due to the conflict between the king and his subjects.
USHA	:	Isn't there anyone else for it?
MUKUNDA	:	Yes. I have sent a proposal to Ramachandra Bhanja of Sarang Garh. He turned it down. He said, "No".
USHA	:	Then, why did you agree?
MUKUNDA	:	As he refused.
USHA	:	He was the most suitable one. He is a prince. Why shouldn't he be the king?
MUKUNDA	:	Of course, he is suitable. He is, however, physically very strong. There is something in him that frightens me when I look at him. He laughs like a monster. His face is comely. But somewhat odd. Frightening. But why should he be unsuitable? As he is suitable, kings are dying one after another giving way to him. I sent him the proposal, but he was unwilling to accept.
USHA	:	He should be the king. Try to decide accordingly.
MUKUNDA	:	He is unwilling. Someone else might be the king. Kingship will never lie vacant.
USHA	:	Look, you shall not agree.
MUKUNDA	:	Why?
USHA	:	I have a reason for it.
MUKUNDA	:	I have many more. Is it your desire?
USHA	:	See darling, nobody prospers on this throne.

MUKUNDA	:	Whoever sits on the throne has to sacrifice his welfare for the welfare of the kingdom. Know it for certain, Ushayinee.
USHA	:	But, you shall refuse.
MUKUNDA	:	Is it the reason? I have refused several times. Of course, not for the reason you apprehend, I shouldn't also.
USHA	:	Why, darling?
MUKUNDA	:	Welfare of the state is prior to mine.
USHA	:	Will you agree?
MUKUNDA	:	'Yes'? Absolute 'Yes' from 'No'?
USHA	:	Why should you say, "No"?
MUKUNDA	:	That is timidity, Ushayinee.
USHA	:	You know that you should refuse. You are acting accordingly. Wherefore timidity?
MUKUNDA	:	I knew, Ushayinee that I should say, "No." I too was saying, "No." Now I understand I should say, "Yes." So, I would say, "Yes."
USHA	:	Well, will you say, "Yes"?
MUKUNDA	:	Definitely 'yes', Ushayinee. But it's a great sin. The throne of Odisha is the sacred seat of my Lord. The King of Odisha is indeed Lord Vishnu, living and moving. All the kings of India come to touch His holy feet with their heads.
USHA	:	Then you should say, "No", shouldn't you?
MUKUNDA	:	No, Ushayinee, it's my duty. So far I have upheld the merit of duty in my life. It's duty and duty only. Duty is very important. My heart throbs in the face of duty. Duty is more significant, Ushayinee. Sometimes, very terrible. When duty calls,

only the Lord can help. I am torn between duty and faith. This duty is very severe, very harsh; faith is very cruel.

(*Curtain*)

SCENE II
The Street.

(*Narayan enters.*)

NARAYAN : How dark it is! Nothing is visible. Ah! I have to do my duty in such a dark night. Even if there is no king, I have to do my duty. What would have happened, had there been a king? The people who pass by will meet with an accident. Oh, who comes here? Take care, bamboos are here.

(*Gopal and Gobinda enter from the opposite direction.*)

GOPAL : Beware, bamboos are here.

NARAYAN : Why are you carrying so many bamboos during this night?

GOPAL : You too are carrying them during daytime? Eh, brother Narayan? Where are you heading to during this dark night?

NARAYAN : Are you out in daytime? Tell me your name.

GOPAL : Make a guess from my voice. Where are you going?

NARAYAN : Leave it. I have the watchman's duty at the palace. I'm going there. It's so dark! Are you Gopal?

GOBINDA : Good guess, eh! Why don't you have twenty ears like Demon Ravan?

NARAYAN	:	Oh! Brother Gobinda. You should have four heads like Lord Brahma. Your tone always varies.
GOPAL	:	If you have twenty ears, each head has five ears. Why can't you recognise my voice?
NARAYAN	:	Eh, Gopal. How playacting (*chha'ta*) you are!
GOBINDA	:	Besides, you we are only three. Where are the six? (pun on *chha'ta*)
NARAYAN	:	Oh, both of you are here. Ok, welcome. Where are you heading to?
GOBINDA	:	We had nothing to do. Just roaming.
NARAYAN	:	You are out at good time! Wait here. Let it rain. If lightning flashes and thunder roars, all your fun will be spoilt. Well, what about that matter? Did esteemed Patra agree?
GOBINDA	:	Everybody – Minister, Army Chief, etc. – called on him yesterday.
NARAYAN	:	What was the outcome?
GOPAL	:	He had not said anything. Who knows what is in his mind? Brothers, last night I had a dream. Esteemed Patra has been the king. He is sitting on the throne. He is being fanned by attendants. All on a sudden I woke up.
NARAYAN	:	Yes, if he sits on the throne, there will be a metamorphosis. Within a year the whole kingdom will be turned into gold. Even though he is not the king, so much has been done.
GOBINDA	:	Eh, it's only a dream. Will the dream come true! The kingdom will be turned

into gold! He will make the impossible, possible. According to the holy book Malika, Kali Yug will come to an end – everything will be destroyed in the year fifteen and sixteen and truth will hold good in seventeenth. That is why king after king are being slain, otherwise who dared touch the king. Destiny will turn around. The kingdom will be turned into gold. During Kali Yug Lord Jagannath will destroy the earth like Lord Parsuram. Come Gopal, let's go. Brother Narayan, when will your duty be over?

GOPAL : Please, be quiet and listen. Who is singing a song?

NARAYAN : He sounds like Gadei. He might be coming. It is his turn now.

GOPAL : You are a genius in recognising voices! Be quiet.

(*Song from background*)

(Song)
Depopulated are villages, fields and forest
Devoid are the prosperous of their treasure
For whom should I live, O dear, O dear?
Kill me, O God and spare me not.

NARAYAN : Here is esteemed Baliarsingh

GOPAL : Brother, when I look at the eyes of this old man, I am out of my wits.

GOBINDA : You can see, though he is old and sans teeth, his voice is still the same.

NARAYAN : He is roaming like a madman.

GOPAL : Is he really insane?

GOBINDA	:	What he has not witnessed! What position he did not have! What does he see now? To where has he declined? Which magnanimous person like him won't be mad? Again, a song has started.

(*Song from background*)

(Song)
In her sons' blood the mother bathes
As brothers are at war
My king is dead in this skirmish,
What a horror did I see, dear?
Some day the earth must rise
Topsy-turvy will be the hills and seas
The sky will sink into the world underneath
Humans and animals will all perish.

GOPAL	:	Here he comes. Greetings, Lord.
GOBINDA & NARAYAN	:	Greetings, Lord.
DHANU	:	Who are you all here in this darkness? What are you doing?
NARAYAN	:	These two have just come. I am going to perform my guard's duty.
DHANU	:	How long are you going to guard? Who are you guarding over? There is headache, if there is a head. Go crazy now, wander about in the jungles and hills, fields and moors. (*exit.*)
NARAYAN	:	This old man has gone crazy since the two sons of King Prataparudra have been killed by Gobinda Bidyadhar.
GOPAL	:	Why shouldn't he? The King has treated them better than his son. What was the old man singing about? Will there be

		deluge? Yes, brother Gobinda, did you know about it before?
GOBINDA	:	Oh! How the old man was singing!
NARAYAN	:	It has started drizzling. Let's go.
GOBINDA	:	Yes, Let's go.
GOPAL	:	What was it? This earth shall roar one day.

(*All exit.*)

(*Curtain*)

SCENE III

The Garden outside the palace of Ramachandra Bhanja
(*Ramachandra Bhanja and his servant Dhurjati are standing.*)

RAMA	:	Well. Are you speaking the truth? Are all asleep?
DHURJATI	:	Yes, My Lord. All are asleep.
RAMA	:	All?
DHURJATI	:	Yes, all.
RAMA	:	Are all the lamps put out?
DHURJATI	:	It is darkness everywhere. Only the lamps are still burning by the roadside. The moon has gone down leaving everything in darkness.
RAMA	:	Can you do it alone?
DHURJATI	:	Yes. Can I not? I can very well do it. This is nothing new, Your Majesty. Those two with this hand – Narasingha and Raghurama Chhotray –
RAMA	:	Well, keep quiet. Take care; nobody should have an inkling of it. Be quiet. Be quiet.
DHURJATI	:	No. who will come to know about it, Your Majesty.
RAMA	:	Swear upon my body.
DHURJATI	:	Should I swear upon Your Majesty's body?

RAMA	: Don't you have trust in me? I have a lot of secrets buried in me. Could anybody know about them, Your Majesty? Eh! Keep quiet. By the by I just told about it. Do I not know?
DHURJATI	: Then why does Your Majesty say so?
RAMA	: Look. If secrecy is out, we are ruined.
DHURJATI	: Be assured. No one will know about it.
RAMA	: Can you do it?
DHURJATI	: Yes, I can.
RAMA	: Hurry up, then. You needn't wait for the Minister. He has told that Dhurjati will go ahead. You see, I have to act it according to his wishes. Proceed.
DHURJATI	: Yes, Your Majesty. (*Exit.*)
RAMA	: Bye. What a horrible night! In one such night Narasingh has a date with Chitragupta. One year after, in another such night, it was as terrible as this, Raghuram went to hell. Hell? Well. What else is there in the fate of a base human being like him other than hell? Today is the third night. Proceed, Dhurjati. Dhurjati is very skillful. He can very well do it. Treachery? It exists for this kind of men. Let's see. I couldn't remind him – to be careful, to maintain secrecy – as secret as a quarrel with wife. It's like a quarrel too, isn't it? Assassination is merely a conflict for me now. Where is that severity? Well, finish the job, Dhurjati. Mukunda will be the king and collect taxes from me as I am a vassal king. Before he asked me for it,

I have sent you to him. Well, Dhurjati, do it well, so that he may not ask for it again. Then, all the taxes of the state will reach this hand – what a fortunate hand you are! You are blessed being in my body. Ramachandra Bhanja is not a beggar, Mukunda, that you would send an offer to me, "Will you be the king?" If I am to be the king, I shall be as such by dint of my own prowess – stupid, not on anybody's suggestion. A king's throne is far above a beggar's seat. I am aware of my duty, Mukunda. Whose footfalls are these! Did Dhurjati return so soon? Dhurjati!
(*Leelabati enters.*)

LEELA : Who is Dhurjati?
RAMA : Oh, Leelabati! Why are you here at this hour of the night, Queen?
LEELA : What are you doing here at this hour of the night, Dear King?
RAMA : I am enjoying the beauty of this horrible night, Queen.
LEELA : The night, of course, is horrible. What is its beauty then that you are enjoying?
RAMA : Fierceness has its own beauty – the beauty that exists in Sage Durvasa's wrath, in Lord Shiva's Tandav, in producing poison during the churning of the seas, in the enjoyment of nectar, and in the beheading of the Demon Rahu.
LEELA : What are you babbling about? Please, listen to me.
RAMA : Did I tell anything incongruous? I am very

	much delighted, Leelabati, that the night though fierce is pleasant. Has he returned? No. No. I mean, go back, Queen.
LEELA	: Who is returning? Where is he coming back to?
RAMA	: No, I told you to go back. A woman has no share in this fierce beauty, dear. The female race is very tender. Women are very weak.
LEELA	: That's true. Let's retire to bed.
RAMA	: Shall I sleep? Dear Queen, proceed first. Retire to bed first. I am just roaming here. Of course, alone. You needn't fear. Needn't worry, too. I am waiting for a piece of good news.
LEELA	: You can have it tomorrow.
RAMA	: No. the messenger has gone to Cuttack. He is getting the message that there will be a meeting of the counsellors. I have been invited. Now, move. Someone is coming. I can hear the sound of footsteps.
LEELA	: I am leaving. Come back quickly to sleep. I'll come again if you delay. (*Exit.*)
RAMA	: Dhurjati!
	(*Minister enters from the opposite side.*)
MINISTER	: No. Hasn't Dhurjati come back, Your Majesty?
RAMA	: No.
MINISTER	: Not, yet?
RAMA	: No. he has gone.
MINISTER	: Gone! Where?
RAMA	: Where he had to.
MINISTER	: Why did he leave so early? He had to depart after my arrival.

RAMA	:	I was telling him the same thing. He said, "No, I shall go earlier." I was forbidding him but he departed. He wished that he would do the work himself. Are all asleep? It is good if he returns after finishing the work. Isn't it the time for him to return?
MINISTER	:	How can I know, Your Majesty? When did he go? He might come back soon. Had he really left? Had he not gone! How horrible assassination is!
RAMA	:	You are right, Minister. Murder is very fatal. I feel disturbed. Homicide! I have never seen it in my life, not even in my dreams. I had no intention, Minister.
MINISTER	:	Why was it done then?
RAMA	:	It has not been done yet. Let Dhurjati return.
MINISTER	:	It's true, Your Majesty. My heart is throbbing too. I feel a void everywhere – in water, on land, in the sky. I take your leave, Your Majesty. I can't stay here any longer.
RAMA	:	Wait, Dhurjati will come back without doing anything.
MINISTER	:	No, Your Majesty. I shall come back in the morning. Let me take your leave.
RAMA	:	Well, go. Dhurjati will come back without doing anything. I too am leaving. If you come across Dhurjati on the way, take him with you. Take care so that he doesn't do anything, Minister.
MINISTER	:	Yes, Your Majesty.
RAMA	:	Well, Oh Night! Before he wears the

crown Mukunda's head will be in my hands. What insolence! How feeble is Mukunda's desire! People are nominating him! People are uneducated. Aren't they nominating me? He, being a mere servant, will be the king when I, being a king, shall be his subject. I shall bow down this head before his throne. How conscientious God is! Minister will make Dhurjati come back. No. How misled the Minster is! It cannot be shown to him. Has Dhurjati finished? Is he returning? Oh! The earth is got rid of a burden today. Let me check. Oh, my heart! Be quiet. Who is this? Whose footfalls are these? Who comes back – Minister or Queen? At this time Queen etc. show their love. Who might he be? Oh, the darkness of this night is very enchanting. Meeting of the court is perhaps not being held.
(*Dhurjati enters.*)
Is it finished, Dhurjati? Fine. Does anybody know anything?

DHURJATI	:	No, Your Majesty.
RAMA	:	Well, it's a good piece of news.
DHURJATI	:	No, Your Majesty.
RAMA	:	What do you mean by 'No'?
DHURJATI	:	Nothing, Your Majesty.
RAMA	:	What? Isn't it done?
DHURJATI	:	No.
RAMA	:	Did the Minister forbid you? Did he ask you to come back?
DHURJATI	:	No.
RAMA	:	Is he not asleep?

DHURJATI	:	No, Your Majesty.
RAMA	:	Is he then awake?
DHURJATI	:	No, Your Majesty. He is asleep.
RAMA	:	Then, is it done?
DHURJATI	:	No, Your Majesty.
RAMA	:	No, Dhurjati. It is done.
DHURJATI	:	No, Your Majesty.
RAMA	:	Why, Dhurjati? What happened? Couldn't you do it alone?
DHURJATI	:	No, Your Majesty. It can't be done.
RAMA	:	Why? What happened?
DHURJATI	:	I dare not. I have a troubled mind. No, Your Majesty. I can't do it?
RAMA	:	What's the matter with you?
DHURJATI	:	A lamp was burning in front of the palace. It was the only one lamp. All else was dipped in pitch darkness. How brilliantly it was burning, as if it was the huge lamp of the temple of Lord Jagannath! As soon as it saw me, it started burning less luminously. While I was looking at it, my heart was throbbing loudly. It ceased to burn. All was lost in thick darkness, Your Majesty, thick darkness.
RAMA	:	Then, it was advantageous, Dhurjati. What else?
DHURJATI	:	Ah, Your Majesty. All lamps are put out. It was the only lamp – Patra, the warrior. Should I put that lamp out? I can't do it, Your Majesty.
RAMA	:	Hush, hush, be quiet. See, Dhurjati, you couldn't do it. How infirm you are!
DHURJATI	:	I could, Your Majesty. It's not a question

		of infirmity. I could very well do it. But, what a cruel work it is! I can't do it, Your Majesty. My hands wouldn't.
RAMA	:	What can you do then? If you attempted, you could know whether you could do it.
DHURJATI	:	No, Your Majesty.
RAMA	:	Keep it in mind, Dhurjati. It is neither your personal work nor mine. It is the job of the state. Do you understand what ruin it is going to bring about if Mukunda is the king? On the one hand, the kingdom is going to dogs. It will be precipitated. Nothing will remain. This soil will even be spoilt. Neither you nor I nor anybody else shall exist. This beautiful land will be a cremation ground. Mukunda is like a meteor. It is inherent in his horoscope, if he is the king, there will be deluge in the kingdom. Famine shall occur. All shall perish. Now try to understand, if I am the king, what will happen to the kingdom. You will be a stakeholder. The name of Dhurjati Barik will be concealed. People will recognise you as Dhurjati Singh or Dhurjati Samant. Go, Dhurjati, go. Try again. You can never avail yourself of this advantage. Will Mukunda ever come to your house to be butchered?
DHURJATI	:	No, Your Majesty.
RAMA	:	Do you realise the advantage?
DHURJATI	:	Advantage is there. He is as if a fruit hanging from the branch of a tree. It is a single stone which is enough to bring it down.

RAMA	:	Then, what? Do you understand?
DHURJATI	:	I understand, Your Majesty.
RAMA	:	You are forgetting yourself, Dhurjati. Remember Narasingh and Raghuram. Mukunda is not greater than them. You don't even understand, if the administration of the kingdom is vested with us, how it will run.
DHURJATI	:	I understand, Your Majesty.
RAMA	:	Then, proceed.
DHURJATI	:	I'll go.
RAMA	:	Go, take care. See that the target is not missed.
DHURJATI	:	There is the old Baliarsingh, Your Majesty.
RAMA	:	Finish him if you get the chance. But Mukunda is your priority. He is the thorn. Do you understand me? He is the thorn on our path. When we tread on the path, it will pierce our feet. There shall be a wound. So, he is the first. Go, Dhurjati, you are being delayed. Do whatever occurs to you first. It is said that the field decides the job. But, Mukunda certainly.
DHURJATI	:	I'm going, Your Majesty. I may be late or fast either. I'll come back after the work is finished.
RAMA	:	The piece of sword is quite shining. When you return, it should be dipped in colour. Keep it in mind, if the kingdom is ours how it will run. Go, Dhurjati.
DHURJATI	:	I'm leaving, Your Majesty.
RAMA	:	Beware, Dhurjati. This time achieve the task and return.

(*Exit Dhurjati.*)

What's now, Minister? Dhurjati shall do it. You could not know about his weakness in the meantime. You shall know that Dhurjati is successful in the very first attempt. There is no way out. I understand that it will be a great blunder if you know about it. But what can be done? Proceed Dhurjati, this time finish the task and come back. Now you have disappeared in the darkness. You live by blood while alive, live in hell after death.

(*Curtain*)

SCENE IV
Forest.

(*Dhanurdhar, Gobinda and Gopal enter.*)

GOPAL	:	We have all gone mad.
GOBINDA	:	Yes, My Lord. We are all crazy. Tell us what to do?
DHANU	:	You will jump about naked if you are mad. Shall I teach it to you? Do as mad people do.
GOPAL	:	They jump about naked.
GOBINDA	:	They talk nonsense.
DHANU	:	You shall talk.
GOBINDA	:	They cry and laugh.
DHANU	:	You shall do the same.
GOPAL	:	What else do they do?
GOBINDA	:	Sing and dance.
DHANU	:	You shall do the same.
GOPAL	:	They wander about here and there.
DHANU	:	You shall do the same.

GOPAL	:	They don't care for food, drink and sleep. They sit in mud and sleep on the ground.
DHANU	:	You shall do the same.
GOPAL	:	Since the last month we have been doing that.
GOBINDA	:	Yes, we have been doing that, My Lord. We have been wandering about in jungles, in hills, in fields, in rivers. We have been roaming, eating leaves and roots.
GOPAL	:	We have been sleeping on the stones and sitting on the ground.
DHANU	:	Yes, dear, you have been doing that.
GOPAL	:	That's why we know that we have gone mad. What more?
DHANU	:	All else.
GOBINDA	:	What's more?
DHANU	:	The other things that the insane do.
GOBINDA	:	We'll do it if you tell us. We won't hesitate. Please, tell us what to do.
DHANU	:	Will you do something big?
GOPAL	:	Yes, we shall.
DHANU	:	Do you see this hill?
GOBINDA	:	Yes, we do.
DHANU	:	Cut this hill into pieces and mix them into the earth.
GOBINDA	:	Yes, we shall. What else?
DHANU	:	Do you see this large river?
GOBINDA	:	Yes, we do.
DHANU	:	What is its name?
GOPAL	:	The Mahanadi.
DHANU	:	Bury this river under the ground.

GOBINDA	:	Yes, we'll do it.
DHANU	:	You can make impossible possible.
GOPAL	:	Yes, we shall. What else?
DHANU	:	Do you know there is anarchy in the state?
GOBINDA	:	Yes, we do.
DHANU	:	Will you rule it?
GOPAL	:	We'll do it. Who will be the king?
DHANU	:	Our king will be the Black Lord in the Temple. Lord Jagannath Himself will be the king.
GOPAL	:	Our king was the incarnate of God. Lord Jagannath Himself.
DHANU	:	You can see the whole state is full of enemies. We have to drive them out.
GOBINDA	:	Yes, we shall drive them out.
DHANU	:	You have to look for them in every village, in every house. Wherever you find a traitor kill him, burn him to ashes.
GOBINDA	:	Yes, we'll do it.
DHANU	:	Demolish their houses and merge them with the soil.
GOPAL	:	Yes, we shall do it. (*Dhurjati enters.*) Who is this, a new man? Brother, are you going to be mad?
DHURJATI	:	I am already mad.
GOBINDA	:	Who are you?
DHURJATI	:	I am the son of a merchant. My business was ruined and I am wandering about here and there.
GOPAL	:	Where are you going?
DHURJATI	:	I am about to do something for a living. If I had money, it would be of help.

GOBINDA	:	What is your name?
DHURJATI	:	Darpa Singh.
DHANU	:	Let's go. Come to that side.

(*All except Dhurjati exit.*)

DHURJATI : It's not convenient. They are three. I could not do it that night. I had to return once. Now I have come to do it. When I raised my hand, I couldn't do it. The sword fell off my hands. I went away to save my life. Fie on this life. The king said that Dhurjati couldn't do it. My parents named me Dhurjati. Of course, it's not a beautiful name. It may be painful to hear it. It's not as tender as Gobinda, Mukunda, Rama, or Shyama nor is it as soft as butter which can't be felt as cotton by hand. But the name Dhurjati is as hard as stone, as sharp as an arrow. It will strike as a bolder when it falls on anything. I couldn't do it. I left both of them. This time I won't return without finishing the task. Am I not worth anything? The king will say that I could not do it – that Dhurjati could not do it. What couldn't he do? Missed only two. Who could not do it? Dhurjati. How can I put up with this scandal? Dear Patra is finished. Who will get him back? Only the old man is left. Let this one exist. Let me go and find out where the old man has gone. (*Exit.*)
(*Dhanurdhar, Gobinda and Gopal enter again from the opposite direction.*)

GOBINDA	:	He is not here. He has gone away.
DHANU	:	Sit down. How did the man mislead us?

	What did he say as his name?
GOPAL	: Darpa Singh.
DHANU	: No. Sarpa Singh. He is a serpent. How peculiar his face is! I was frightened to look at it. Gopal, sing a song.
GOPAL	: (*Song*)

Days are passing, Oh God, in this world
We take refuge under your feet bold. (*Refrain.*)
You are our saviour in sun or rain
We meditate on you during rest or action.
You kill all wicked, foster all good,
In fair or foul you save all world.

(Curtain)

SCENE V
The Street of Sarang Garh.

(*Minister and Army Chief of Odisha enter.*)

CHIEF	: Isn't it a blame on Ramachandra Bhanja that the dead bodies of the two assassinated princes are found in the territory of Sarang Garh?
MINISTER	: I have been wondering about it since long, dear Commander?
CHIEF	: No, something must be done about it before long.
MINISTER	: Certainly.
CHIEF	: Only a simple 'Certainly' won't do. Command me and I shall follow. This kind of nefarious activity should be stopped forthwith. Who will be willing to be the king of your state under these circumstances? To be the king means to

cut one's head first with his own hand and put it under the throne and then sit on it. Dear Patra being a warrior, generous and amiable, has consented. Who else would be prepared under these circumstances to wear the poison dipped crown of Odisha? His consort is forbidding him. Kith and kin are protesting. Yet he is as resolute as a hill, because it's the call of duty. That is why it is our duty, Venerated Minister, to keep the throne secure for him, to open a field for him to govern.
(Narayan enters.)

MINISTER : What's the matter, Narayan?

NARAYAN : The king of Sarang Garh went to the palace. As he couldn't meet you, he is coming here.

MINISTER : Let him come. Is he perhaps looking for something, Chief?

CHIEF : Might be. Everybody on earth is looking for something. Is anybody free from searching? Well, Narayan, is he far off or nearby? Oh, he is coming.
(Ramachandra Bhanja enters.)

MINISTER : Welcome, oh king! We have to labour hard.

RAMA : But all your labour is in vain.

MINISTER : Is anything not found?

RAMA : No, I told you earlier that you need not search for it in my kingdom.

MINISTER : Yes, you were telling it from the beginning.

RAMA : Did you see it yourself?

MINISTER : We could see it now.

RAMA	:	All of you can search elsewhere. You can't find anything here; why anything? There is no possibility of anything. Are you leaving today?
MINISTER	:	Yes, we will. We are going tomorrow, if not today. There is no need to linger here.
RAMA	:	Well. All of you please come to the palace. We'll return together.
MINISTER	:	Please proceed.

(All except Narayan exit.)

NARAYAN	:	This kingdom is not so bad. But there is no happiness here. As mind gets fresh if one wanders around the Garh, no such thing is happening here. Only legs get sore. Then one or two comes here and detains you for an hour. Let me leave now. It's a long way off.

(Banambar enters.)

BANA	:	Hey, haven't you gone yet? My God, how could you stay here leaving your family at home? I cannot do it for even a day.
NARAYAN	:	I have come here on duty. How can I go back unless the work is finished?
BANA	:	What your job now? Looking for dead bodies, as you had said that day? Have you ever played "Du, Du"? How can I say it publicly? Looking for dead bodies – playing on the drum? I see, you'll let the cat out of the bag.
NARAYAN	:	You were telling that day that you would tell me something. Why didn't you say it?
BANA	:	Hey, I'm telling you so many things. Yet you say that I'm not telling you anything.

MUKUNDA DEB | 39

		What a man you are! Shall I tell you about big things like an elephant or a horse? What an important work!
NARAYAN	:	Yes, the king is gone. He is not coming back again. They have killed him.
BANA	:	Eh, who did it? How did he do it – with blows or slaps? If he was hit with slaps, his cheeks might have turned red like hibiscus. His cheeks as yellow as champak might have turned as red as hibiscus.
NARAYAN	:	No. killed him. Put an end to his life.
BANA	:	Put an end to life? Whose? Yours?
NARAYAN	:	I'm living. How am I killed?
BANA	:	Yes, you are right. You are alive. Then whom? How did he kill him? Tripped him or hit him on the head? Eh, hitting the head with slight blow? His head might have turned into stone.
NARAYAN	:	Slew him.
BANA	:	Eh! What did you say? Slew him? He might have fallen down as a tree when it is felled. Cut his legs? He might have fallen down.
NARAYAN	:	No. His throat is cut.
BANA	:	Oh, he is saved! His legs are not cut. He might have fallen down.
NARAYAN	:	You have seen it, haven't you?
BANA	:	Me? My liver turns into water as I hear about it. Watch out. There was whispering about it for a month. I am unable to sleep. Well, let's go.
NARAYAN	:	Please wait a little.

BANA	:	No, dear. I have a lot of work to do. I am not as free as you are, so that I can enjoy leisure with you. I am leaving.
NARAYAN	:	Let's go. I shall accompany you.

(*Curtain*)

SCENE VI
A Chamber in Sultan's Palace.

(*Suleman, Dillir Khan and Hasan Khan are seated.*)

HASAN	:	May I say that the Nawab of Banga is unwilling to pay taxes?
SULEMAN	:	You know what to tell.
HASAN	:	I'll tell that the Nawab of Banga is unwilling to accept the suzerainty of Delhi.
DILLIR	:	Please tell, Hasan Khan, the Nawab of Banga shall write out the reply you are going to submit to Badshah Akbar and you'll get it by heart and reproduce it like the vomiting of a patient suffering from indigestion. You are a clever man. You know what to tell. Why do you ask so much?
HASAN	:	Why do you say so, esteemed Nawab?
SULEMAN	:	Please listen to me. The matter is, we are not going to pay taxes.
HASAN	:	What is your reason for it?
DILLIR	:	What is your reason for asking for it?
HASAN	:	Tax is our due. Moreover, there is the command of the Badshah.
SULEMAN	:	Ha! Ha! None of these is correct?
HASAN	:	How is it? Isn't tax our due?
DILLIR	:	The answer to both of your questions is the Nawab of Banga is quite possibly unwilling to pay taxes to your Badshah.

HASAN	:	Why?
SULEMAN	:	One who governs the state shall collect taxes.
DILLIR & HASAN	:	Exactly.
SULEMAN	:	Then?
DILLIR	:	Then, the Nawab of Banga governs the state but taxes will be collected by the Badshah of Delhi. How fantastic!
HASAN	:	Have you forgotten that as a Nawab of the Badshah you are collecting taxes on his behalf?
DILLIR	:	Oh, this is why you have come to collect taxes. How fantastic!
SULEMAN	:	A Nawab of the Badshah? How is it, Hasan Khan?
HASAN	:	Hasn't the Badshah won this territory?
SULEMAN	:	Can anyone demand taxes from another after only one defeat in the battle?
HASAN	:	Shall I tell this to the Badshah?
SULEMAN	:	You may. If you want to say more, you may say that the Nawab of Banga doesn't expect such undue disrespect from the Badshah of Delhi in future.
HASAN	:	Well, is there anything more?
SULEMAN	:	Well, yes, Hasan Khan. Akbar belongs to our religion. It is agreed that he is powerful, competent and clever. As the state of Banga is stolen from a Hindu king, the empire of Bharat is a treasure stolen from several Hindu kings. As he considers himself a victor we too feel the same. The state of Banga has never

		accepted the dominance of the Badshah of Delhi. Therefore, now the Nawab of Banga should see that neither Badshah Akbar nor his delegate like you trespass the territory of Banga.
HASAN	:	If it so happens?
SULEMAN	:	In that case, tell him that cannon balls would remove those feet from the battle field.
HASAN	:	Well, esteemed Nawab, I'll say so. Are you then ready for war?
SULEMAN	:	We'll not surrender our state to the enemy without war.
HASAN	:	Well, I take your leave. (*Exit.*)
SULEMAN	:	Dillir Khan, we'll face another war.
DILLIR	:	Yes, the Servant of Allah. Akbar will again invade us.
SULEMAN	:	His thirst will never be quenched if he doesn't vanquish Banga. Then?
DILLIR	:	We have to get ready.
SULEMAN	:	Akbar has a vast army, Dillir. The independence of small states is at peril before an empire. A vast army!
DILLIR	:	All of them will not come to invade Banga.
SULEMAN	:	Of course, not. They will defend their capital, guard their territory. The more one wins, the more huge one's empire is. The more huge the empire, the more huge the enemy.
DILLIR	:	Yes, the Servant of Allah.
SULEMAN	:	Then, send the message to the Commander to leave the northern territory. Repression

of the dacoits! It will be done later. Let's save ourselves first, shan't we?

DILLIR : All right, the Servant of Allah. I'll send the message today. May I leave now!

SULEMAN : Akbar! You are a great riddle in politics. Nations are won by force. But it's manoeuvre which is your weapon now. You claim that you are building an empire without war. Do you know, Badshah, how many prosperous states you have ruined; how you have burnt down the entire Bharatvarsha by dint of the fire of quarrelling brothers; how you have separated wives from their husbands; how you have made sons revolt against their fathers; and set friends against one another? You may not reap its consequences, but your children and grandchildren as well as the entire Mughal race will suffer its consequences. Suleman is not a weakling, Akbar. I have Afghan radiance in my heart, Afghan prowess in my arms, and Afghan blood in my veins. I won't submit without war. I am not a slave to your schemes. If you like, you my try your strength against me. Suleman Shah is the independent Nawab of Banga. Suleman will be victorious in war if Akbar alone or with the support of a vassal king challenges him to fight. Freedom of the state of Banga will be written in Mughal blood. All this bloodshed is futile, Akbar.

(Curtain)

ACT II
SCENE I

A Meeting of Mukunda Deb in the Palace of Odisha.

> *(Mukunda Deb is seated on his throne. Minister, Army Chief, Dhanurdhar and Hasan Khan are seated.)*

Danseuse : (Song)
Bloom all over the forest, oh, blossoms,
Dance gently, oh, breeze,
Sing sweetly in groves,
The song of your life
Oh, cute humming bees. (Refrain)
Spring has come down to earth
Cuckoo sings enchantingly
Golden waves ripple in life
The earth, as if, is rolling in joy.
The river is flowing with a sweet murmur
The forest is babbling with a rustle
The gem of humans is rolling like droplets
Of love in the golden throne. (Exit.)

MINISTER : Badshah Akbar is the greatest enemy of this country, Mughal Ambassador. He is unwilling to face the Feudal kings in the battle field. Its reason, of course, as he says, is his desire to desist from bloodshed. You know, Ambassador, if he had tried his strength in war, he would not have been the ruler of such a vast empire. His skill in maneuvering is the reason of the downfall of Bharatvarsha. The king of Odisha would not consciously help such an enemy, Ambassador. Please, go back.

HASAN	:	Mughal Emperor is now in adversity. So, he prays for help.
CHIEF	:	Maybe. But the king of Odisha is averse to help him. Do you know, Hasan Khan, how the Mughal Emperor is tormenting the people of India? What ruin has he brought about for the Indians? If necessary, the king of Odisha will raise arms against Emperor Akbar. The bosom of the motherland will be flooded with Mughal blood. The future independence of India will be built on the heaps of Mughal dead bodies. There is no question of help.
HASAN	:	The Mughal Emperor has heard that the king of Odisha is very generous. He never hesitates to grant refuge to a person who seeks it.
MINISTER	:	It's true, Ambassador. We may prefer to be ungenerous, and deprive the refugee of shelter to offering help to Akbar.
HASAN	:	Will you turn down the request of a person in adversity?
MINISTER	:	We'll kick out such prayers.
HASAN	:	Then, shall I carry this message from the court of the Gajapati King of Odisha that the Odias may prefer to be mean, hateful, ungenerous; will deprive the shelter-seeker of shelter; put the man in adversity in more hardships; even when the most powerful emperor of India prays for help, he will turn down his prayer and pay a deaf ear to the ambassador's proposal?

MUKUNDA	:	Certainly not. The Minister and the Army Chief of Utkal may not honour the proposal of the Emperor of India. I'll do it with all my might, and give shelter to the refugee. You needn't worry, Mughal Ambassador, as long as a single coin is left in the treasury of Odisha, as long as a single soldier is left in the army of Utkal, the shelter seeker Akbar may remain assured of help of Utkal.
MINISTER	:	No. Emperor, it's a blunder.
MUKUNDA	:	It's not a blunder, Minister. An Odia may be banished from his state, sacrifice his fortune, beg at others' door yet he shall not deprive the shelter-seeker of refuge.
MINISTER	:	We don't agree with you, Emperor.
MUKUNDA	:	You may not. Then, you are not going to sacrifice your fortune. You shall not beg at others' door
MINISTER	:	Then you will be deprived of our cooperation, Your Majesty.
MUKUNDA	:	I agree. I'll depend on the few soldiers of Odisha who like to share the fate of Patra, they know long since, and assure shelter to the refuge seeker.
CHIEF	:	In that case, no soldier of Odisha shall support you, Emperor.
MUKUNDA	:	May not. I shall relinquish the crown and proceed alone. Yet I shall not turn down the refuge-seeker. Come, Hasan Khan, even though the Mughal Emperor may not get the support of the fabulous wealth of Odisha, as well as the support of the

		vast army, the king of Odisha alone shall offer his power and assistance.
DHANU	:	Your Majesty!
MUKUNDA	:	Dhanurdhar Baliarsingh! What do you want to say, old General?
DHANU	:	Are you really going, Maharaj?
MUKUNDA	:	I have to, old General. What else? Bid me farewell. Please, come, Mughal Ambassador.
		(*Mukunda and Hasan Khan exit.*)
DHANU	:	Good bye, Minister, Dear Chief. I admit that Akbar is our major enemy; foreign invaders are hateful because they have subjugated India. I abhor Mughal Emperor Akbar as an enemy but when he prays for help from our race, he is a refugee for me and my bosom friend. I had once sacrificed my life for the glory of Mother Utkal. I'm now at the fag end of my life. Yet it's my glory that our Emperor is going and therefore, let me go with him. Good bye, Minister. Farewell Dear Chief. (*Exit.*)
MINISTER	:	It's a matter of grave concern, Chief.
CHIEF	:	But what is the way out? Will the king come back?
MINISTER	:	Certainly not. Until the work of the Mughal Emperor is not finished.
CHIEF	:	Then?
MINISTER	:	Protect the kingdom. Let the crown be on this throne as it is, as long as the king is not back. Our state is our priority; human race comes next. Let's defend our state

first. We have to do it at the cost of our life. We are not generous; we are not noble. Narrow nationalism is our first love. Our first duty is our kingdom's defence. We have a heavy burden on our shoulders. There are enemies in and out of the state. Still we have to keep our state safe. We are narrow minded, no doubt, but we are ready to sacrifice our life for our narrow-mindedness.

(*Curtain*)

SCENE II
The Yard outside Ramachandra Bhanja's Chamber.
(Ramachandra and Leelabati enter.)

LEELA	:	Dear, is a wife the maid servant of her husband?
RAMA	:	No. wife is the better half of her husband, Leelabati.
LEELA	:	Then, is there anything secret between a husband and a wife?
RAMA	:	Nothing, Leelabati.
LEELA	:	Then open your heart to me. I am a woman, though weak by name, but not by nature, Oh, Lord of my Life. Wife is the other half and the sharer of piety. It's a matter of great regret that I could not be so yet, as Sita was to Rama, Damayanti was to Nala and Shakuntala was to Dushyant. Please accept me as your other half not only during your meals and sleep, comfort and leisure, dream and consciousness but also with regard to your duties, your

	thoughts in the inner recesses of your heart. Your graceful face has become pale; the shine in your eyes is dull; and the smile in your lips is fading; dear. Please, tell me, 'why'. Why do you look so dull, miserable, and worried? If possible, I shall try to redress your worries. I may not be anything to you but as we have joined our hearts with the holy knot on the altar of our wedding, I shall share your sorrows, and add my sighs to yours. Husband is the Lord of his wife. In order to offer my worship to my husband, I shall sacrifice myself.
RAMA	: I know, Leelabati, you can better do it. But I have no such miseries that you can remove; no such suffering in my heart for which I shall seek your help to reduce them. It's now midnight. Go, Queen, have rest. How fierce is the night's horror for the delicate body of a woman! I can't think of it, Leelabati. Please, go. Why do you delay?
LEELA	: You shall accompany me.
RAMA	: I shall come a little later. Here, someone is coming. Can't you hear the footsteps? Please, go.
LEELA	: Please, come early. (*Exit*.)
RAMA	: This must be Dhurjati. Well, this Dhurjati is as deadly as a poisonous serpent for the society. He is like a snake hiding among the sweet flowers. Here, he comes. What crooked sight he has! What vicious

glances of Shakuni he has! He must have finished the job. Still he has another task to do. (*Dhurjati enters from the opposite direction.*) Dhurjati is the first useful person for me in my life. Oh, Dhurjati. Come. Are you successful this time?

DHURJATI : Yes, Your Majesty.
RAMA : No?
DHURJATI : No, Your Majesty. It is done.
RAMA : Done. Well, you could do it this time. Had you done it last time, you would not have to do it again. Finished? Could anyone know it, Dhurjati?
DHURJATI : No. my hands were not willing at first, Your Majesty.
RAMA : Did it move this time or refused like the previous time?
DHURJATI : Compelled to move.
RAMA : I, too, didn't want it at first, Dhurjati. When Mukunda survives, it's not safe for us that the Minister should live as he knows about it. What do you say, Dhurjati?
DHURJATI : What is there in saying? The work is done.
RAMA : It would have been a blunder if the Minister had survived.
DHURJATI : Why?
RAMA : You don't understand. When he knows everything ---.
DHURJATI : I too know it, Your Majesty.
RAMA : You not only know it, but also you are doing it. You are the half of my life, Dhurjati. You have done well. The Minister

has become the victim of the sword he had dedicated for Mukunda. How misled man is! One who thinks ill of others shares the same misfortune. This is life. One moment man dominates the earth, the next moment he too is dominated by someone else. Well. You have done good, Dhurjati. I'm now secure. Nobody can get an inkling of anything if neither you nor I reveal it.

DHURJATI : It is total ruin if the secrecy is shared by three. It is said that a goat becomes a dog in three mouths.

RAMA : One mouth is finished. What else is left?

DHURJATI : Nothing else is left, Your Majesty.

RAMA : We are free of one burden. I was in constant fear, Dhurjati. Now I am free from worries. Night has advanced. Go and sleep peacefully tonight. I, too, am leaving, Dhurjati. (*Exit in opposite directions.*)

(*Curtain*)

SCENE III

The Camp of Mukunda Deb during his expedition to Banga.

(*Mukunda Deb, Dhanurdhar and citizens are present.*)

DHANU : These are the people, Your Majesty, who are willing to sacrifice their life for you.

CITIZENS : We are ready to sacrifice our life for the king.

MUKUNDA : Who are these, General? Soldiers?

CITIZENS : We are not soldiers, Your Majesty. Ordinary citizens. But now we will obey

		the commands of our Maharaj and fight the enemies in the battle field.
MUKUNDA	:	Why do you so desire, Citizens? You are to live peacefully in cities and villages. Why do you unnecessarily come into the horrors of the battle field, stain your hands in human blood, and sacrifice your peace of life? Why? For whom?
CITIZENS	:	We'll do it and are ready to do much more. But we won't let our King go to war alone.
DHANU	:	Your Majesty, these are ten thousand citizens from the villages. When they learnt that the king was going to war alone, all of them swore that they will wield weapons, learn the technique of warfare, be at the battle front protecting the king, and if necessary, will sacrifice their lives. This oath spread among the citizens in the frontier villages like wild fire. The farmers collected their ploughs, washer men their axes, black smiths their hammer and came forward. They all assembled under the flag of Maharaj. Ladies of the inner precincts handed over swords to their husbands; loving mothers decked their sons in military outfits and sent them to the King. They have all dedicated their lives to their king, Your Majesty.
CITIZENS	:	We have all dedicated our lives to you, Your Majesty.
MUKUNDA	:	Do you mean they are ten thousand, General?
DHANU	:	Yes, Your Majesty.

MUKUNDA	:	Oh, the ten thousand sons of Mother Utkal, you have sacrificed your peace and happiness for the glory of the nation. The soldiers of this state shall stay back to protect the state, and you are going to protect the glory of the kingdom on the foreign ground. Blessed you are, Oh, village folk. Come, let's now pray for our victory and proceed on the path of duty.
CITIZENS	:	Victory to our King! (*All except Gobinda and Gopal exit.*)
GOBINDA	:	If these ten thousand people learn warfare, they will fight well.
GOPAL	:	They may. But can they fight like soldiers?
GOBINDA	:	Are common people born as soldiers? These common people like us become soldiers and indulge in battles. Who are we fighting?
A SENIOR	:	Is it Suleman Shah?
GOPAL	:	No. it's Nuselas, isn't it? These Muslim names are very awkward; they can't easily be articulated.
GOBINDA	:	Are the Muslims human beings like us?
GOPAL	:	Are they tigers, and not human beings? Haven't you seen a Muslim?
GOBINDA	:	Have you seen one?
GOPAL	:	I may not have seen one but can't I recognise one?
GOBINDA	:	How can you know if you have not seen one? An elephant apple has six pieces if you have not seen one.
GOPAL	:	If it has six pieces it will maintain all its

		properties. Will it not taste sour? Will it not feel smooth to hand?
GOBINDA	:	One piece more will add to its sour taste.
GOBINDA	:	Similarly, a Pathan is a human being. He might have a tail more or a head less. There may be a minor difference.
GOPAL	:	Haven't you heard that Demon Råvana had ten heads?

(*Dhanurdhar enters.*)

DHANU : Look, Gobinda and Gopal. The Emperor had to participate in this war for the sake of the glory of our state. We have to bid farewell to our motherland as long as we have not come back. We are ten thousand in all. But these are all uneducated. They can learn within these few days. That is our faith. The enemy soldiers are not only more in number but also they are better skilled and better educated. Even then we have no misgivings, no fear, no apprehensions in our mind. The Lord is our saviour.

(*Curtain*)

SCENE IV
The Street.

(*Minister and Army Chief of Odisha enter from opposite directions.*)

MINISTER : Have you come, Chief? I was going to meet you. Have you done it?

CHIEF : Yes, I have done it. Barabati will be protected by Koni Samant Singhar in your absence. He will have ten thousand soldiers with him. They can move elsewhere if there is need.

MINISTER	:	What about the South?
CHIEF	:	Purandar Jagadeb will be stationed there or wander there as he pleases with ten thousand soldiers. Five thousand soldiers will be spread all over.
MINISTER	:	Then, we will proceed with the rest fifty thousand soldiers. We have the message that Maharaj has now crossed the Ganga and is entering the state of Banga. There may be war before long.
CHIEF	:	Before we join him? The ten thousand villagers have joined the Maharaj, they are new recruits. It's a matter of grave concern, esteemed Minister. The Muslims are very intrepid as a race.
MINISTER	:	You have to proceed immediately. It's far off. It may take you at least fifteen days or a little more.
CHIEF	:	The soldiers are ready, esteemed Minister. We needn't delay. We are leaving now. Let's go.
MINISTER	:	Good bye, Chief. We'll meet in this fort when you return.

(*Curtain*)

SCENE V
The Bank of River Ganga.
(*Mukunda Deb and Dhanurdhar are seated.*)

MUKUNDA : After the whole day's clanging of weapons and ferocious sounds of cannons, the murmur of the river is enchanting, isn't it General?

DHANU : It is a strange transformation, Emperor.

MUKUNDA	:	It's like the birth of nectar after the churning of the seas. Today is the tenth day of the bright fortnight of Phalguna. The moonlight is clear. Crores of moons are shining on water. The festival of the spray of coloured powder might have started today. The city of Cuttack might have been covered with coloured powder.
DHANU	:	We have here started to play with liquid colour. We have dipped ourselves in human blood from head to toe. How cruel is this massacre! Even then the Muslims are very powerful. They are as strong as they are skillful.
MUKUNDA	:	That is true, otherwise, they would not have adorned the holy throne of Delhi which was once the seat of Yudhishthira and King Vikram Aditya. Now the Muslims are controlling the destiny of Bharatvarsha as they were once dominating the half of Europe.
DHANU	:	Suleman is also a good warrior, O King. It is heard that he is as good as Darrius, Chengiz Khan, and Timur Lang.
MUKUNDA	:	Did you see, General, how they brought about a transformation? We never anticipated it. Who knows, what will be the outcome of this war?

(Guard enters.)

GUARD	:	Your Majesty, a Musalman has come to see you. He says that he is the General of the Musalman Army.

DHANU	:	General of the Muslim Army? With soldiers?
GUARD	:	Nothing serious. He said, it's a …
MUKUNDA	:	What is his intention?
DHANU	:	Does he want a meeting?
GUARD	:	He said so.
MUKUNDA	:	Well, let him come. Is he Muslim General, Kalapahad? Let him come. There is no harm.
DHANU	:	No, there is no harm. Let him come. He might be our enemy in the battle field. He is our guest now. That's why, he is a friend.
MUKUNDA	:	Let him come. Allow him to come. Escort him. (*Guard exits.*) I apprehend, General, our glory may be tarnished. It's not about you and me. It's the question of the glory of Utkal. If Odias are defeated in this war, Muslims can assess our strength and then it will be easy for the foreign invaders to attack us.
DHANU	:	Yet, it is as if our condition is doubtful. We may very well be defeated. But what else can we do? Truce? So early?
MUKUNDA	:	Here he has come. (*Kalapahad enters.*) Please come, General. What brings you here to this stranger? It's our good fortune.
KALA	:	We have a certain purpose. My visit is not without a purpose, Emperor.
MUKUNDA	:	Please, reveal it.
KALA	:	I have come here with a proposal, Emperor.
MUKUNDA	:	What is it?

KALA	:	I have come here to wish you victory.
MUKUNDA	:	How is it? You should wish for your victory first. A wish is not a proposal. It is an affair of the mind, only a feeling.
KALA	:	Let me disclose it clearly. I wish to help you, Emperor.
MUKUNDA	:	To help us!
KALA	:	Yes, Emperor, to help you.
MUKUNDA	:	We are quite ready to accept your help, General. But it is not the right time now.
KALA	:	Well, when?
MUKUNDA	:	After the war.
KALA	:	You may not need our help then, Emperor.
MUKUNDA	:	We'll not accept it at that time, General.
KALA	:	Let me clarify myself a little more, Emperor. I am ready to fight in this war on your behalf.
MUKUNDA	:	Will our Commander then fight along with Suleman? Is it your proposal or the Nawab's?
KALA	:	It's my own proposal, Emperor.
MUKUNDA	:	Are you going to desert the Nawab?
KALA	:	I will.
MUKUNDA	:	It is not the right proposal, General. It's not possible. Please, go back.
KALA	:	Shall I go back? Please keep it in mind that it won't be beneficial to you, Emperor. Your victory is certain if you accept my help. Shall I then go back? On the one hand, it is my return and your defeat, and on the other hand it is your acceptance of my help and your victory as a consequence; the choice is yours, Emperor.

MUKUNDA	:	I have made my choice, the General of Banga. I don't mind my defeat as a consequence of your return. The Odia may be vanquished, oppressed and ruined; the brilliant face of his motherland may be tarnished; his heroic blood may disfigure the foreign soil and fields, but he shall not take recourse to perfidy. He shall not destroy his enemy with the help of somebody from his enemy's side. He will not desire for the glory of victory for his motherland by means of falsehood and treachery. You should know, General, we are not fools to be greedy of victory by any means. We are not blind for the luxury of war. It's not our strategy to win war by unfair means. Please go back to your camp, Mughal General.
KALA	:	Is it your final word?
MUKUNDA	:	Yes, it is. Farewell till tomorrow.
KALA	:	We'll meet tomorrow. In the battle field?
MUKUNDA	:	Yes, in the battle field. We shall meet there.
KALA	:	Well, we'll meet in the battle field. But remember, Emperor, our meeting in the battle field will be our final meeting. We'll meet in the battle field. I'll see the battle strategy of the Odias in the battle field. I'll see how the Odias fight, how he does not deviate from the path of justice in spite of defeat and humiliation. I'll gather all Muslim forces against you in the battle field. I'll apply all Muslim strategies

against the Emperor's sense of duty. I'll see how the Odias as a race are.

MUKUNDA : Well, you may better do that, General.

(*Curtain*)

SCENE VI
The Garden outside the Palace of Saranga Garh.

(*Leelabati enters while singing.*)

LEELA : (Song)
Alas! Oh, Moon, fade from the sky
How cruel you are! (Refrain)
Will you roam happily in heaven
Leaving the lily in the pond afar
To suffer the pangs of separation?
She would have bloomed to the full
and danced in the wind gleefully
Honey bees would have hummed around
Raining pollen dusts on her.
All hopes are dashed,
She will close her eyes in intense sorrow,
She will not laugh, nor dance in the wind,
Sleep eternally with tearful eyes.

I don't know why there is such discontent in me. It cannot be satisfied even for days to come. The scene of the battle field! No, women are frail. Oh, the venerable Lord of my life, a woman seeks her husband's affection, begs for his love. He is also the sharer of his virtues. Husband and wife are bound by means of a sweet chord on the altar of religion. What attraction I do feel in that holy bond, dear!

(*Ramachandra Bhanja enters.*)

RAMA	:	Leelabati!
LEELA	:	Yes, dear.
RAMA	:	What were you doing? Why are you alone at this hour of the night? Go home.
LEELA	:	Doing nothing. Just bothered by meaningless thoughts.
RAMA	:	Haven't you stopped thinking? Always thoughtful! What thoughts!
LEELA	:	What a sense of duty King Mukunda Deb has, dear! He gave up an empire, forfeited his claim on the throne. Yet he is the glory of the kingdom. He is facing the enemy because of his principles. He is the only stream of laughter amidst eternal sorrow of Mother Utkal. He is the only blossom in the desert of Utkal.
RAMA	:	You may say that he is the only verse of poetry amidst all black stains. You seem to be speaking in poetry. Go home.
LEELA	:	The aliens have been in possession of this holy Bharatvarsha for long. Mukunda Deb is facing these alien enemies in the battle field. The soldiers of Odisha are shedding invaluable blood in the dreary battle fields for the honour of the state, to safeguard its sovereignty. Oh, Lord of my life, I am your partner in life, yet I am frail as a woman. I cannot share your duties when you will wield weapons against the enemies.
RAMA	:	You can very much do it, Leelabati, go.
LEELA	:	No, Dear, why should I go alone? I am not so strong. Please take me with you.

RAMA	:	No, go home. The night has advanced. Go to sleep.
LEELA	:	Please, come with me, Dear. You shall accompany me.
RAMA	:	No, Leelabati, I have a meeting now. It's the affair of the state. You first proceed.
LEELA	:	Meeting! Your first meeting in youth was with me, this unfortunate woman. At this ripe age, come and have a meeting with me, Dear. (*Both exit.*)

(*Background voice*)

FIRST	:	Oh, somebody's voice is being heard.
SECOND	:	The king is perhaps waiting.
FIRST	:	Maybe. We are not late, of course.

(*Shikhi and Manai enter from the opposite directions.*)

SHIKHI	:	Oh! There is no one here. Whose voice could you hear, Manai?
MANAI	:	Couldn't you hear the voice? Somebody was talking.
SHIKHI	:	That was our own voice, Manai. A voice is audible, if we move stealthily. Silence has its own voice.
MANAI	:	Here, the king is coming. I hear somebody's footsteps.
SHIKHI	:	It's the sound of our own footsteps. Hasn't quietness its own noise?

(*Ramachandra Bhanja enters.*)

RAMA	:	You have come in time. Am I late?
SHIKHI	:	We have just now arrived, Your Majesty.
RAMA	:	Are you ready to proceed?
MANAI	:	We are ready, Your Majesty.
RAMA	:	Tell Kalapahad to help us. Either he should

		send an army, or come himself. The whole of North Odisha! From the Subarnarekha to the Ganga! It's not a small territory.
SHIKHI	:	No, Your Majesty. It's not less.
RAMA	:	Do you know the path? The secret path?
MANAI	:	Yes, Your Majesty.
RAMA	:	Guide him along that path, very secretly. Let no one get an inkling of it. Tell him in addition – he will surely be …. how shall he be benefitted by fighting on behalf of the Nawab of Banga? However, the job will be easier here when the war continues there.
MANAI	:	Yes, Your Majesty.
RAMA	:	Mukunda might not have returned.
SHIKHI	:	Yes, Your Majesty.
RAMA	:	The army might not have returned.
SHIKHI	:	Do you sense, Manai, how advantageous it is? You are right, Your Majesty.
RAMA	:	They might not get the news of this battle.
MANAI	:	Yes, Your Majesty.
MANAI	:	How easy the work will be, then! Apprise him with everything. Of course, with secrecy. If the enemies get a hint of it, there is no hope of anything. We beg your leave.
RAMA	:	You may leave. First of all, bring him with you. Secondly, do everything secretly.
SHIKHI	:	(*Both of them rise.*) Be assured about it, Your Majesty. (*Both of them exit.*)
RAMA	:	This is somehow settled. The Muslims are very much thirsty of occupying Odisha.

They have not done it so long because they could not do it. They have not got such an opportunity. It's no less an offer – from the Subarnarekha to the Ganga – it's not a small temptation. Kalapahad must come. With his help Mukunda Deb will first be punished. What to speak of punishment? It's total ruin. Ruin. Ruin. Ruin. Oh, Dear Queen, you are making me soft, making the stone melt. Leelabati is the Queen in the inner apartments of a palace. She has no role in administration nor in winning territories. Destruction! It's destruction! The goal of my life is fixed. Oh, my heart, be courageous! It is not a minor thing – what Dhurjati could not accomplish – an assassin like him. Destruction of Mukunda Deb. Well. The possession of the throne of Odisha. Well. Then the vast army of Odisha! How marvellous! To drive out Kalapahad then is just a trifle. It's a very nice proposal. What to speak of proposal only! It's the outcome which is certain. It may be quite possible. The truth may come out someday – the emperor of Odisha – how nefarious! I asked Dhurjati to come. I could have done both the tasks together – winning the throne of Odisha and clearing the scandal of homicide. The Minister knew about it. He is finished. Dhurjati is left. I asked him to come. What happened? Could he sense it? My doubts!

	My guess! Maybe. If he is finished, I am fully assured. No. I have to finish him. There should be no delay. He always comes in time. Why is he late today? (*Dhurjati enters.*)
DHURJATI	: Who is late, Your Majesty?
RAMA	: You are.
DHURJATI	: No, Your Majesty. I'm just in time.
RAMA	: No, Dhurjati, you are late, too late. Blood may gradually become cold.
DHURJATI	: What do you mean, Your Majesty?
RAMA	: Dhurjati, you have killed all – Narasingha, Raghurama, and the Minister.
DHURJATI	: Yes, I have, Your Majesty. I have carried out Your Majesty's commands.
RAMA	: You a great sinner, Dhurjati. Bring the minister back immediately.
DHURJATI	: Why do you say so today, Your Majesty?
RAMA	: Bring Narasingha and Raghurama back.
DHURJATI	: Your Majesty, I have not spared Mr. Patra knowingly. I have not spared the old Baliarsingh knowingly.
RAMA	: Now follow the path of Narasingha, Raghurama, and the Minister. (*attempts to kill him.*)
DHURJATI	: Please, spare me, Your Majesty. I'll bring Patra's head to you and …
RAMA	: No, Dhurjati, I want your head … (*attempts to kill him.*)
DHURJATI	: No, Your Majesty. (*Dhurjati flees. Rama follows him.*) (*Background voice*) Go, Dhurjati, be in hell for good.

(*Screams of a dying person is heard from the background.*)

(*Curtain*)

SCENE VII
A battle field in Banga.

(*Suleman is lying on the ground wounded.*)

SULEMAN : Dillir! Dillir, you didn't even combat this final moment. No, it's not possible. Not possible in this life. I wish I saw you once, Dillir. Oh, how painful it is! Asthe powerful ruler of Banga, I was proudly saying that I am not the Nawab of Banga; I am the Badshah of Banga. Oh, on this lonely bed of sand –my life is coming to an end. The name of Suleman will be eliminated here. Well, let me get ready. Suleman, the Badshah of Banga is at the death's door. No. No. Ready to breath his last. Why did nobody come? Well, it's impossible. Let the name of Suleman be buried in this deserted field. Oh, – without the knowledge of the whole world –

(*Mukunda Deb enters.*)

MUKUNDA : No. it's not possible, Badshah.
SULEMAN : Why? Who are you? Dillir?
MUKUNDA : No, Badshah. It's Mukunda Deb, the king of Odisha.
SULEMAN : My enemy! Come forward! (*stands up with sword in hand*)
MUKUNDA : I have no weapons with me, Badshah. I am a friend now. Hold yourself.

SULEMAN	:	*(falls down on the ground again)* How? Oh, it's very painful. Dillir! Dillir!
MUKUNDA	:	There is no one here, Badshah. Please tell me what you want.
SULEMAN	:	Why are you treating an enemy like this, oh, Emperor? Has the war stopped?
MUKUNDA	:	Yes, it is going on. *(placing Suleman's head in his lap)* Oh, Muslim warrior, the Badshah of Banga, you are in much pain. You are in great suffering. Your body has been severely injured. You are bleeding profusely. Please have a little rest. The wounds on your body speak about your heroism. Please have a little rest, Badshah. The wounds on the body is identity of a warrior. Please rest a while without worries. You will come round soon. Don't worry about the war. War, of course, goes on. When you are a little better, both of us shall rise up again. Here, a Muslim is coming towards us. Well, he has come in time. *(Dillir Khan enters.)* Are you Dillir Khan?
DILLIR	:	What is this, the Servant of Allah?
SULEMAN	:	Dillir!
DILLIR	:	Have you wounded the Badshah, eh Hindu? Oh, Allah! Now pay for the consequences of your action, eh Kafir. *(tries to attack Mukunda.)*
SULEMAN	:	*(obstructing)* Calm down, Dillir. *(falls down on the ground again.)* Oh!
DILLIR	:	The Servant of Allah!
SULEMAN	:	Dillir, I have heard that the Odias are

		generous. I thought that they might be like Mahmud of Ghazni or at best like Babur of Kabul. Oh! I am unable to speak. It's very painful. Is it very painful?
MUKUNDA	:	Please don't talk much, Badshah. Have rest. Is it still painful?
SULEMAN	:	No. I had no idea of Odias. I never dreamt that they might be so generous, Dillir. Oh!
MUKUNDA	:	Please, talk less, I told you. It will be more painful.
SULEMAN	:	No, Maharaj, I am feeling better. Remember, Dillir. Remember the Emperor of Odisha. He is as heroic as generous.
DILLIR	:	(*kneeling down*) Please, excuse me, Maharaj. I have made a mistake due to my ignorance.
SULEMAN	:	Remember, Dillir. Oh!
MUKUNDA	:	Please, talk less.
		(*A soldier enters.*)
SOLDIER	:	The war has come to an end. The Muslim soldiers are retreating.
MUKUNDA	:	Well, keep quiet.
SOLDIER	:	Army Chief is pursuing them.
MUKUNDA	:	Go back, soldier. (*To Suleman*) Do you feel a little better?

(*The soldier exits.*)

SULEMAN	:	A little better. You are the victor now, Maharaj.
MUKUNDA	:	Please listen to me, Badshah. Be calm for a while. Well, Dillir, prepare for shifting the Badshah to the camp.
SULEMAN	:	What can be done, Maharaj? The camp is very far off.

MUKUNDA	:	Well, (*To Dillir*) call that soldier. (*Dillir exits*) You can have rest when you go to the camp. You need rest now. You will get well with good rest.
SULEMAN	:	Well.

(*Dillir enters with the soldier.*)

MUKUNDA	:	Bring the palanquin, soldier. Hurry up.
SOLDIER	:	Maharaj! (*Exit.*)
MUKUNDA	:	How long will it take to reach the camp, Dillir?
DILLIR	:	It's not very far away.
SULEMAN	:	Oh, you might have cut off this head of mine, Maharaj. You might have drenched the ground with my blood. No, it won't happen now. I am dead now. How can I be alive?
MUKUNDA	:	You will survive.
SULEMAN	:	Why?
MUKUNDA	:	You will rise up again for war.
SULEMAN	:	Well.
MUKUNDA	:	Again, as my enemy.
SULEMAN	:	Well.

(*The soldier enters.*)

MUKUNDA	:	You can then drench the ground with enemy blood, if necessary. Ae you back, soldier?
SOLDIER	:	Maharaj.
MUKUNDA	:	Hold him, Dillir.

(*Both of them lifted Suleman up.*)

SULEMAN	:	It's a great pleasure, Dillir, to have an enemy like this. Glory be to the Odias. Farewell, Maharaj. You are a great warrior, noble and generous, at the same time.

(*Dillir and Suleman exit.*)

MUKUNDA	:	What were you saying, soldier? Are the Muslims vanquished?
SOLDIER	:	Yes, Maharaj.
MUKUNDA	:	Vanquished?
SOLDIER	:	Yes, Maharaj, vanquished.
MUKUNDA	:	What about the General?
SULEMAN	:	He was pursuing them.
MUKUNDA	:	Whom?
SULEMAN	:	Those retreating soldiers.
MUKUNDA	:	What about the Muslim General? He has also fled. *(Dhanurdhar and soldiers enter from the opposite direction with Kalapahad as a prisoner.)* Oh, here is the General. Are you here as a prisoner?
KALA	:	Yes.
MUKUNDA	:	What kind of treatment do you expect from me?
KALA	:	As the victor desires. I don't beg for my life from the enemy king.
MUKUNDA	:	Set him free, General.
KALA	:	I'll accept my freedom if am suitable for it. I mustn't beg for it.
MUKUNDA	:	You are the most suitable, General. *(Dhanurdhar sets Kalapahad free.)*
KALA	:	Well, what is my duty now?
MUKUNDA	:	You may retire to your camp, General.
KALA	:	Farewell, then, Maharaj. (*exit.*)
MUKUNDA	:	The Muslim General is a great warrior. He does not care for being taken as prisoner. He treads like a lion. The war has come to an end now. Let's return to our kingdom, General. Our motherland is in danger.

	Minister and Army Chief might be feeling helpless. Motherland! Ah, motherland, how sweet you are! Please, reveal your enchantingly beautiful image embodied in your forests and hills, rivers and fields, villages and countryside. Let me once address you as "Mother" resting myself in your loving lap. Oh, my Motherland! (*Noise nearby*) What is this noise about, General? The voice seems familiar. I haven't heard it long since. The voice sounds as sweet as the sweet notes of the harp. Who is there? (*Minister and Army Chief enter.*) Minister and Chief?
MINISTER	: Maharaj, you have left the crown there. The throne remained vacant. It is not our action; it's the inspiration of Utkal Ma. May the head adorn the crown again. (*puts the crown on Mukunda's head.*) Soldiers, Chant victory slogans for the Maharaj.
SOLDIERS	: Victory to Maharaj.

(*Curtain*)

ACT III
SCENE I
The chamber of Kalapahad.

(*Kalapahad, Shikhi and Manai are seated.*)

KALA	: Is it from the banks of Ganga to the Subarnarekha?
MANAI	: Yes, General, the entire territory.
KALA	: It is the northern territory of Odisha. How far does the southern territory spread?

SHIKHI	:	From the Subarnarekha to the Godavari.
KALA	:	It's a very vast country. Have the Odias occupied such a large territory by their own efforts? From the Ganga to the Godavari. This is north and that is south. It is one country. Why north and south? Well, we will help you. You are telling me to hurry up. Why? Why so quick?
MANAI	:	It is the opportune moment.
KALA	:	Let me know how. The first opportunity is that the king of Odisha is far away along with the Minister, Army Chief, and the army. It's a great opportunity, of course. What is the next opportunity?
SHIKHI.		The second opportunity is that the rains are coming; rivers and canals will be full. Hills and forests will be impassable. You should reach before that.
KALA	:	It is true. But Mukunda Deb will return as soon as he gets the message. What do you think in that case?
MANAI	:	No, General. we will pass through a very secret path; through the dense forest and hills. There is no possibility that anyone can know about it. Please, get ready. Arrange your soldiers. Collect necessary weapons. Please, don't delay. We take leave of you now. We will guide you when you are ready.
		(*Shikhi and Manai exit.*)
KALA	:	It's a nice proposal. I am destined to get what I have been looking for since long. It is impossible to occupy Odisha without

the help of the Odias. To enter Odisha is very difficult. Odias are no less in military skill and heroism. Heroism! Oh, how heroic Mukunda Deb is! That day he turned me down, saying, "No, it is not possible." What humiliation for the General of Banga! The victory flags of the Muslims are flying all over India. Only Odisha is an exception. Now I have the assistance of Ramachandra Bhanja. It's a gift of God. Oh, what humiliation that day! "I choose your return even if we are defeated because of that." Now your defeat is certain. You have done right. I admit that you have valour, and skill in warfare. Yes, that day I was a prisoner. It was an irony of fate. You have set me free, Mukunda Deb. I'm grateful to you for that. Kalapahad may be mean, detestable, and savage but never ungrateful. No, I did not beg for my freedom. One who begs for mercy may be grateful. To set the prisoner free without being approached is generosity of the victor. It is his reward. What more? You will see what Kalapahad can do in the battle field. How he is going to avenge his humiliation. Yet, it should be secret. Let me see, Daud Khan can very well do it. I'll start a war by instigating the king of Manipur. Then, there will be truce with him. Then expedition to Odisha will be safe and secret.

(*Dillir Khan enters.*)

		Oh, Dillir Khan! What is the news?
DILLIR	:	I have no message to convey but I have come to collect news, Your Highness.
KALA	:	To collect news? You have very bad news, Dillir. The condition of the country is deplorable. On the one hand, the Mughal Emperor is our enemy. The southern territory is terrible. The dauntless Maharaja of Odisha is ready with an army, all prepared. We were defeated that day because of his prowess and military strategy. It's a great blemish for the Afghans. A great infamy for the Muslim show of strength. It is heard that the king of Manipur is about to declare war. He is moving his army on the border of Banga. What might be worse news than this, Dillir?
DILLIR	:	No, Your Highness. The war threat is coming from Manipur at this hour of peril. It is as if God wills that the Afghan kingdom shall be in ruins; Afghan Badshah shall be in danger; the history of Afghans shall be wiped out from the pages of history of Banga. But no, we have to work with patience, to protect the kingdom from the attack of the enemies, and keep up the name and fame of the Afghans as far as possible.
KALA	:	That's true. Afghans are not so weak that that they can be petrified by a little scream of Akbar or Mukunda Deb or the king of Manipur. We have to organize our army, appear in the battle field and keep up

the honour of the state according to our might.

DILLIR : Even then it's a matter of grave concern, Your Highness, that on three sides there are enemies. We may comfortably guard one front; guarding two sides may be a little more difficult but if the enemy is present on all the three sides, it will be quite impossible to tackle them. The predicament of the Afghan empire in Banga is like that. It's not only one front but the other three sides have to be protected. There is no use in pondering over it. We have to do it.

KALA : I'm thinking of who will guard the fronts, Dillir Khan. We have, of course, been defeated in the previous battle, but we have not surrendered our freedom. Mukunda Deb, the friend of Akbar, has won the battle and is camping on the border of Banga. He may again attack if he gets the message from Delhi. Why may? He must. Who knows? Mughal Badshah may himself come. Therefore, soldiers should be in readiness in the kingdom. We also need more soldiers to fight Manipur. It is the same for Islam whether Akbar wins or Suleman wins. But if the king of Manipur wins, will it not be a blemish for the kingdom, for the race? It will be a blot on the glorified Islam religion, Dillir. He might be generous, but we are bound by religion, therefore narrow-minded.

DILLIR	:	Yes, Your Highness. We have to make serious preparation for the war with Manipur. The Badshah will not deviate from our suggestions. To safeguard Banga, preparation is necessary not only for the South but also for the West and the East.
KALA	:	Might be more, Dillir Khan.
DILLIR	:	Yes, Your Highness. It is a religious war. We have to sacrifice every drop of blood, lakhs of soldiers, and spend enormous money. I propose that Badshah should stay in the capital and protect south-western territory. If necessary, he may declare war. If assistance is needed, I may be left with him. You should proceed to suppress Manipur.
KALA	:	The proposal is not bad, Dillir. Well, why don't you come to Manipur with me?
DILLIR	:	No, Your Highness. Here, we have two enemies. Is it desirable to leave the capital vulnerable?
KALA	:	No. Never. Your proposal is right. We have to convince the Badshah with this proposal. It is the empire for the Badshah and religion for us. It is his duty to protect the empire; our first duty is to protect religion. We will be answerable to God if we err, Dillir. It is a very solemn duty. This duty is very dreadful.

(*Curtain*)

SCENE II
The path in the garden.
(*Ushayinee along with a handmaid enters.*)

HANDMAID : (SONG)
Who is swimming
in the water of the pond
 in the darkness of the night
as the wind is blowing gently;
while singing joyfully with all his heart
as sweet as the murmur of a stream
the song of the wild flowers ? (refrain)
The moon, decked in diamond, hears the song,
The stars too hear in the sky,
The leaves of trees, the creepers of the garden,
Are lost in the charming strain,
These sweet notes tinged with pollen dust
Change into enchanting songs
The touch of dust quivers notes of a flute
Come soon and listen to it.

USHA	:	Do you think, dear, that a man is singing in this pond with a sweet murmuring note of a stream?
MAID	:	No, dear elder sister. Why should I think so? The water is producing a murmuring sound.
USHA	:	Then, why did you say that someone is swimming?
MAID	:	It is in the song. I am not singing it of my own nor did I compose the lyric. It is also in the song that the moon, the jewel of the night, is listening. Does the moon really

		wait to listen to this song? It is in the lyric. Can it be true?
USHA	:	Who says it, dear? The moon might not be listening to your song. You, of course sang it. You are not the first person to sing the song. Many people might have sung it before. The moon might have listened to the song sung by the first singer, whether it is a male or a female. Why won't he listen when the heart is in anguish?
MAID	:	He is so far off. How can he hear, Elder Sister?
USHA	:	He will hear whatever might be the distance. Won't his heart be troubled, when someone is crying for him? Whatever might be the distance, he is his own. It is said that even if the elephant roams in the forest, he belongs to the king. (*A servant enters.*) Bamshi, where are you going so hurriedly?
BAMSHI	:	Your Highness, Kalapahad is coming.
USHA	:	Who is Kalapahad?
MAID	:	It's a hill. How does it come?
BAMSHI	:	No, elder sister, Kalapahad is coming. The whole kingdom is agog with the news that Kalapahad is coming. People have come with this message from a long distance. He has burnt down many villages on his way. He has destoyed many gods and temples. People from village to village are obstructing him with sticks, bows and arrows, axes, and spears but they are unable to withstand him. He is coming

	with tremendous force. People say that he is coming to the fort. Who knows what he is upto. Goddess Ma Chandi, you are our refuge.
USHA	: Are you frightened, Bamshi? You needn't fear. Go and convey the message to Samantasinghar. Barabati is not such a fragile fort that the General of Banga will break into it. This fort is made up of the blood of the Odia heroes. Its foundation is on the dead bodies of Odia soldiers. Go, Bamshi and convey the message to Samantasinghar. You have nothing to worry, nothing to be afraid of. Go.
BAMSHI	: I beg leave of you, Your Highness. It is not auspicious that the enemey enters when the king is absent from the kingdom and the soldiers and the Chief of the Army are away,
MAID	: When is the Maharaj expected, Your Highness?
USHA	: He will return soon. He is returning from the battle fields of Banga. He is camping on the banks of the Ganga on his way. The Muslims have availed of this opportunity and has entered the kingdom. It's very bad time for us. (*A maid servant enters.*) Have you come with any news, Parimala?
PARIMALA	: A lady messenger has come from the Queen of Saranga Garh.
USHA	: Well, bring him in. Is she a lady messenger? Or a man messenger?
PARIMALA	: I'll guide her in, Your Highness. (*Exit.*)

USHA	:	The Queen of Saranga Garh is a good person, Dear. While we had been together during our childhood, we were eating, sitting, sleeping and wandering about a lot. We are born at the same place. She is a little senior to me. She brought me up as her younger sister. Of course, I am far away. I cannot pay back her debts in my life. (*A messenger enters.*) Have you come from Saranga Garh?
MESS	:	Yes, Your Highness.
USHA	:	Is the Queen well?
MESS	:	(*hands over a letter*) She has given this letter to you. She is not quite well. You can know everything from this letter.
USHA	:	Does she remember me yet? What is the matter with her? (*goes through the letter*) Empress, I brood over the childhood memories with you and recall them with joy everyday. You are now great by the grace of God. May God bless you! I have written this to you now when I think it is highly necessary. Maharaj is now away. He has come out with flying colours and is glorified for it. He is also decorated with national honour. It is a matter of great concern that the Muslim enemies are present in the state. It is the duty of all the subjects to defend the nation. The king of Saranga Garh is going to meet the Muslim General, Kalapahad in the battle field.

We will be safe if Kalapahad is defeated and retreats. Otherwise, it will be a great concern for worry. How can we be happy and fortunate when the state is in peril? I am not writing anything more. We need to be very careful now.

Yours wellknown,

Leelabati

USHA : Leelabati, who is known to me before! Isn't Leelabati well, messenger? 'The childhood memories since long!' . You have combined the present memories with it, sister. Kalapahad is in the state now. We have now harsh duties. It is true that Ramachandra Bhanja may be the enemy of the king of Odisha. He is a nonentity in Odisha. It is the right duty of the subjects. He does not have adequate number of soldiers. We have to send ten thousand soldiers to him. I'll look to it first. Dear friend, get ready. Come, messenger, accompany me. Get ready, Parimala. Convey the message to all. Smantasinghar will defend the Garh from outside. We will all be ready inside the fort. We may sacrifice our life but we'll not surrender the Garh to the enemy. Things may not go that far. Ramachandra is capable - if he gets ten thousand soldiers. We must still be ready. Blow the war bugle. Assemble all the women of the fort. Go. (*All exit.*)

(*Curtain*)

SCENE III
The camp on the bank of the Ganga.
(*Mukunda Deb is in meditation. Minister, Army Chief, Dhanurdhar are present.*)

DHANU	:	If that is the case, please send for a Kahalia, Esteemed Minister.
MIN	:	A man has been sent to call him. He might come any moment. Did you tell, soldier, that Kalapahad had gone to the South?
SOLDIER	:	Yes, Your Highness.
CHIEF	:	Was he defeated in the battle? How long did the battle last?
SOLDIER	:	Two days.
DHANU	:	Samantasinghar was commanding the soldiers.
SOLDIER	:	Yes, outside the fort.
CHIEF	:	Who was inside the fort?
SOLDIER	:	The Queen.
MIN	:	Is the Queen prepared for the battle inside the fort? Has Kalapahad not broken into it?
SOLDIER	:	No, Your Highness.
MIN	:	Is he pulling down the temples, gods and goddesses? (*Kahalia enters.*) Look, Kahalia, play on the *kahali* very hard. Sing this – The enemy is inside the state. May the Maharaj rise from his meditation! Do you remember?
KAHALIA	:	Yes, Your Highness. The enemy is in meditation. May the king's kingdom be in ruins!

CHIEF	:	Oh, no. 'The enemy is inside the state. May the Maharaj rise from his meditation!' Repeat.
KAHALIA	:	'The state is in the enemy'.
MIN	:	Excellent! Oh, no. Say, "The enemy is inside the state."
KAHALIA	:	"The enemy is inside the state."
MIN	:	'May the Maharaj rise from his meditation!'
KAHALIA	:	'May the Maharaj rise from his meditation!'
DHANU	:	Repeat everything once more.
KAHALIA	:	'The enemy is inside the state. May the Maharaj rise from his meditation!'
MIN	:	Play this on the *kahali*.
KAHALIA	:	(*plays on the kahali*) 'The enemy is inside the state. May the Maharaj rise from his meditation!'
MUKUNDA	:	Who is the enemy?
MIN	:	Kalapahad, the General of Banga, Maharaj.
MUKUNDA	:	Is he in Odisha now?
MIN	:	Yes, Maharaj. It is a grave concern for Odisha. Kalapahad along with his soldiers is now demolishing temples and deities in Odisha. He went to attack Barabati fort. There was war for two days. He has been defeated and has moved to the South. There is Neelachal Dham of Lord Jagannath. Moreover, Ramachandra Bhanja is openly declaring himself as the King of Odisha. It is rumoured that Kalapahad is helping him in this regard. It is also heard that ten thousand soldiers of

		Maharaj have joined him. The whole state is in tumult.
MUKUNDA	:	Kalapahad! Is he that Kalapahad, whom we met on the banks of the Ganga that evening, and in the battle field he was released by the Old General himself? That Kalapahad? Why is he in our kingdom?
DHANU	:	It is heard that Ramachandra Bhanja has invited him. It's not impossible, Maharaj. It may be very much possible. Nothing is impossible for Ramachandra Bhanja.
MIN	:	What is our duty now, Maharaj?
MUKUNDA	:	We have to return to our kingdom immediately. First of all, we have to warn the king of Sarang Garh. If necessary, fight him. Then, Kalapahad. All of you get ready. Hurry up, as soon as possible. Commander, please ask the soldiers to get ready. Minister and General, look after all preparations. We need not even take a draught of water here. The state is our first priority and our comforts come next. Please proceed.

(*All except Mukunda Deb exit.*)

I told you Kalapahad to meet me in the battle field. We have met once. We may meet again. That is right. Why do you target the religion? What harm has the temples and deities done to you? You are doing a great blunder, Kalapahad. Ramachandra Bhanja, you are also doing a great blunder by inviting Kalapahad to our state, if at all you have done that.

The desire to be the king of Odisha! You might have satisfied that desire by killing me, or by banishing me or by imprisoning me. Why did you, commit this blunder? Muslims are inside the state of Odisha, in the holy land of Utkal. Kalapahad, we will again meet in the battle field. Is it the war between Hindus and Muslims, between the Vedas and the Quran? No, it's a delusion. There is no difference between Hindus and Muslims. The Hindus are warriors and generous, and Muslims are heroic and even more generous. Both are as if two flowers on one sepal. They are swinging in the flow of the wind. It's another delusion. The war is not between Hindus and Muslims. It's war between the Odias and the alien enemies, between the king of Odisha and the General of Banga, between Mukunda Deb on one hand and Kalapahad on the other. My motherland is in jeopardy. Help us, Oh Lord Jagannath! There is not even a day's peace in the state when trouble has risen up in the state. There is again the threat of bloodshed even when the horrible stain of blood has not been wiped out from the bosom of green fields. Oh, Mother Utkal! Oh, Lord Jagannath!

(*Curtain*)

SCENE IV
The path to the Garden.
(*Leelabati along with her handmaid enters.*)

LEELA : (SONG)
Why did you, Oh Sun, fade from the sky,
And darkness covered the earth?
Why did you steal from the plants
their uncommon golden beauty?
Gently blows the wind in the garden,
ripples rise on the water of the pond,
shadows of trees standing on the banks,
as if secretly meets the water's heart.
Trees see their beauty
on the mirror of the water
You have stolen, Oh Sun, that luxury
Still roam in the expanse of the sky.

I think, Sulakshana, that such an evening is entering into my life. Nothing makes me happy. I too don't understand what makes me unhappy. Happiness and sorrow are alike for me. Does it happen so while life comes to an end? Is my life coming to an end, Sulakshana?

MAID : Why, Your Highness? You have still a lot of life left. What is there in such thoughts? Happiness and sorrow are a part and parcel of man's life. Does anyone on earth spend one's life in complete happiness or complete sorrow?

LEELA : No, Sulakshana. It might certainly be not true. There might be some mystery in it. It's not against Mukunda Deb; it's against the motherland. How is it? No, it must

	be against Kalapahad. I cannot believe anything else. The wife is the religious partner of the husband, partner of his life, certainly not a maid servant. Can it be possible?
MAID	: I hear somebody's voice, Your Highness. Somebody is coming.
LEELA	: What did you say, Sulakshana?
MAID	: I said that somebody is coming. Can't you hear a voice?
LEELA	: Yes. Somebody might be coming. Let's go.
MAID	: All are coming in this direction, whether night or day. Yes, they are coming, Your Highness. We can't go away. Let's hide, shall we?
LEELA	: Well. (*Leelabati along with her handmaid hides behind a tree.*) (*Shikhi and Manai enter in disguise.*)
SHIKHI	: Manai, hurry up. We can't meet the king if we are late.
MANAI	: Shall we be blindfolded? It's true that nothing comes to my view; but only these flower plants. Please wait brother, let me pluck a champak flower. (*Banambar enters.*)
BANA	: Eh, it's total ruin. Don't pluck. Don't pluck. Who are you?
SHIKHI	: We are very close to the Maharaj of Odisha.
BANA	: Oh, close relation! Whose? The Maharaja of Odisha! Why have you come here, eh? To pluck flowers! How romantic you are! Isn't your Maharaja engaged in war?
MANAI	: Yes.

BANA	:	(*Sarcastically*) Then, flowers are very much needed, aren't they? Lord Kamadeb has also killed several enemies with his flower arrows. What a big thing a battle is! Two men will be standing by his either side. And what more? They will have heaps of flowers with them.
MANAI	:	Yes, what more?
BANA	:	Eh, what more? As if nothing more! How clever both of you are! That's why, you are close to the Maharaja of Odisha. How will you fight if you gather flowers?
SHIKHI	:	Then?
BANA	:	(*Humorously*) One of you will fling flowers one after another – one, two, three – (*Making onomatopoeic sounds of showering blows*). Another will also do the same – flower after flower (*Repeating onomatopoeic sounds of falling things*). Then you can call it a battle.
MANAI	:	It seems that you know battle tricks very well.
BANA	:	(*Sarcastically*) Eh, telling a tall thing! I have fought as many battles as I have hairs on my body. My body has turned red with blows of flowers, head has many scars. Play with flowers but don't touch *kewda* and *ketaki* flowers. Oh, my dear father! If one them touches you, your body can't thrive; it will be scarred with wounds and blood will flow out. Flowers like hibiscus, mogra, malati and muchukunda are suitable for battles. Ah, if you pluck two mogra flowers, I shall fight with you.

SHIKHI	:	We fight with swords, not with flowers.
BANA	:	Eh, what did you say? Sword? Ah, me, Sword? From flowers to swords! Dear me! Let me go. What is it? With sword? (*Exit.*)
MANAI	:	Let's follow him a little, Shikhi. (*Both exit.*) (*Leelabati comes out from the side of the tree along with her handmaid.*)
LEELA	:	No, it is not, Sulakshana. These are the close personnel of the Maharaja of Odisha. Why would they come here? As human mouths speak false things, human ears listen to false things too. That's why, it is said that we should not believe in what the teacher says but only in what you have seen with your own eyes.
MAID	:	It's true, Your Highness. If we believe in what we hear, we won't disbelieve thunder roars, music of the flute, throbbing of a heart. It may all be true. Possession of a ghost, chanting of tantras, turning around of a winnow may ne true. Even falsehood may appear as true. Then, rumbling of thunder is not true. There is water in the clouds. When they are stirred, they will produce murmuring sound. How can it produce rumbles? Maybe, Your Highness. We have to leave this place. Those two men are coming here. Maharaj is also coming with them.
LEELA	:	Well, come with me. Let's go, Sulakshana. (*Both exit.*) (*Ramachandra Bhanja along with Shikhi and Manai enters from the opposite direction.*)

RAMA	:	Did you check yourself in the mirror? Is it right?
SHIKHI	:	Yes, Maharaj.
RAMA	:	Do they dress like this, Manai? Has your turban been a little bigger!
MANAI	:	It's big, Your Highness.
RAMA	:	Had your belt been a little more red, Shikhi!
SHIKHI	:	It's exactly red, Maharaj.
RAMA	:	Will they detect it? Well, tell where you will stay.
SHIKHI	:	Very close to him.
MANAI	:	We will do as ordered.
RAMA	:	Say again. Let me check it.
SHIKHI	:	We will stay very close to him.
RAMA	:	If he goes anywhere?
MANAI	:	We too will be with him.
RAMA	:	Well, go on telling, Manai.
MANAI	:	We'll be with him always. If Your Highness wins, it's good. We will arrest him there. If, God forbid, he wins, then we'll do the needful then and there.
RAMA	:	Yes, it's the right thing. It's the battle field. There is no distinction between kings and subjects, great or small. Dress as ourselves and kill them with our weapons or dress as themselves and kill them with their weapons. The result is the same. Remember, Shikhi, we win virtue, if we kill or are killed in war. God has said that the sinners are to be destroyed. It has been written in the *Markandeya Puran* that the wicked demons are killed. Go and finish

	this holy work. See that the war comes to an end tomorrow.
SHIKHI	: We beg your leave, Your Highness. Tell Manai, 'Victory to Maharaj'!
MANAI	: Victory to Maharaj!
	(*Both exit.*)
RAMA	: This is the golden opportunity. Mukunda has come to attack in the right moment. Now Kalapahad is busy in his work. Of course, the state will suffer. He might be destroying temples and altars. We are saved if he returns with that much. What shall he do more? What might be his desire? Is it religion? In that case I am assured about the state. His Muslim soldiers are well educated, and competent. It's enough. Well, Shikhi and Manai are better than them. These two can accomplish the impossible what the combined army of Sarang Garh and Banga cannot achieve. Well, Ramachandra Bhanja will be the king of all Odisha. Veer Shree Gajapati Goudeswar! How high is my destiny! I shall be the Emperor rising from a simple king. What is fate? It's the outcome of physical prowess and intense cleverness. Let me realise my own glory. Still I have a lot of hurdles on my way. I have to get over them at first. I have invited Kalapahad into the state. I'll check how the Muslims care for justice. Well.
	(*Curtain*)

SCENE V
The Battle Field.

(*Suleman is standing.*)

SULEMAN : You have committed a great blunder, General. You have let the state into peril. You have surrendered the glory of the state to the enemy. You have allowed the victory flag of the Afghans to be soiled. Now such a horrible act here; so secretly done, without my knowledge. You are demolishing sacred Hindu temples and deities in the villages and cities. It's a great blunder, General. Muslim soldiers are disorganised in the battle field. It is not possible for me to organise them today. I shall do it tomorrow as far as possible. Let me return to the camp today. No I shall visit the Maharaj in this battle field today.

(*Four Odia soldiers enter.*)

SOLDIER 1 : There is one more Pathan here.
SOLDIER 2 : Kill him. Kill him.
SOLDIER 3 : Catch hold of him first.
SOLDIER 4 : Go, go away, Pathan, as your brothers are fleeing.
SULEMAN : Maharaj! This demon is looking for Maharaj.
SOLDIER 2 : Make him a ghost first. Then he will say about the ghost.
SOLDIER 3 : I am swinging my sword.
SOLDIER 4 : There is no use in killing a small fry. Leave him.
SULEMAN : Why are you bothering me? Tell where the Maharaj is.

SOLDIER 1	:	Again, speaking about Maharaj! Be quiet.
SULEMAN	:	You won't tell me anything. Let me try elsewhere. (*exit.*)
SOLDIER 2	:	Let's pursue this man, brother.
SOLDIER 3	:	Let's go. (*All exit.*)

(*Shikhi and Manai enter in disguise.*)

SHIKHI	:	Is there any doubt of losing this time, Manai?
MANAI	:	No. where is the chance of doubt? If there is any doubt now, then the heaven and the earth are in doubt. The sky and the hell are in doubt. You and I are doubtful. If we are to be defeated, we will be defeated. It is more dangerous than death if we lose while winning. Well, winning and losing are the same. Need we bother about winning or losing? The matter is, when we have undertaken a job, we should not leave it halfway. Moreover, there is the reward. The state of Athagarh. It's not a small thing. Let's go, Shikhi. What else? We are a little late for our job. We should catch hold of Mukunda Deb immediately. We needn't delay.
SHIKHI	:	If there is defeat, the other thing is to be taken care of, Manai. Where is the question of catching?
MANAI	:	No. there is no question of catching. I remember – to kill him. We should catch him first, then the question of killing arises. Let's not delay, Shikhi. Come fast. (*Both exit.*)

(*Mukunda Deb enters.*)

MUKUNDA : I can hear the din of victory from all directions. It seems like the dying voices of these blood drenched fallen soldiers in their death bed. I have several times heard victory roars in the battle field. I have often been thrilled by them. Unique currents of joy have overflown my heart. But, today this heart is torn into pieces. Utkal, my motherland, you have washed your bosom with the blood of your children. You have filled your loving lap with the dead bodies of your children. What an ugly image! How horrible your apparel is! It is as sorrowful to watch as it is hateful. Is it victory? Is it for this the people of the world are anxious, excited and concerned? Oh my God! How irresistible is man's desire! Oh, my dear subjects of my state, you are to be looked after with filial affection. But you have forgotten all the joys and sorrows, desires and ambitions and lying on the ground in eternal sleep. I tread on your dead bodies. How cruel! How hard hearted! How stupid! Didn't you see this scene with your own eyes, General? Didn't you see it Dhanurdhar Baliarsingh? What is this bloodshed for? For the throne of Odisha? It is better to be a beggar. No, Ramachandra Bhanja! There is a limit to cruelty. I cannot see my subjects, who are to be looked after with affection, to be lying in eternal sleep? Kingdom? It's very insignificant! Throne?

It's meaningless! I admit that I am the ruler of this vast territory of Odisha. Be off with the crown. Let it lie on the ground with the dead bodies of my subjects. Be off with my sword. I feel free. Hands and head are free. My heart is without any burden.
(*Shikhi and Manai in disguise re-enter.*)
Here are two soldiers. Their hands are dipped in brothers' blood. Their heart is grief-stricken. Come, soldiers, behold this pathetic scene.

SHIKHI : Don't delay. Be quick, quick.
(*attempts to attack.*)

MANAI : Be quick.
(*Suleman enters from the opposite direction.*)

SULEMAN : Watch out!
(*attacks both of them.*)

SHIKHI : I'm dying Manai.
(*falls down dead.*)

MANAI : Oh, I'm dying.
(*falls down dead.*)

MUKUNDA : Badshah, how could you be here so suddenly? Strange are the ways of God! I was brooding on the meaninglessness of life. Just at this time there is this plan for my murder. Now life and death are the same for me, Badshah. (*raising his sword*) Do you see this sword, Muslim warrior? It has bathed in the blood of a number of warriors in the battle field. I can finish the drama of my life with it easily. But, no. There is some more time left for it. I'll never hand over the throne to Ramachandra Bhanja, the traitor. I myself offered the throne to him. He was unwilling to accept. He said, "No." Now, he plans to kill me. Then, come out openly, Ramachandra Bhanja. This treachery is unbearable.

(*Curtain*)

SCENE VI
The ground outside the camp in the battle field.

(*Ramachandra Bhanja enters.*)

RAMA : Lucky fellow! Escaped twice. Last time it was treachery. This time it is misfortune. It is as if like a calamity, a hurricane, that descended swftly and clasped Mukunda and vanished. The only benefit is that everything is revealed. Everything now will be done openly. Still the man is very lucky. But no more. As long as Mukunda did not care for death, he could manage to evade death. But it his oath is now which is the enemy of his life. To rescue the state from treachery means to offer one's own head to death. It's fine. Fighting does not mean tryng one's physical strength, Mukunda. It's a trial of intelligence, a tug at cleverness. I needn't depend on others any longer. I'll sharpen my sword now. This is not violence. It's self defence, pure self defence. It's an effort to free oneself from the other who openly stands as an enemy. But, it should be done in the battlefield. It does not look nice if done elsewhere. People will blame me. They may say that it's an assassination. But, no, in the battlefield. It's time now for the preparation for war.

(*Raghunath and Sadashib enter from the opposite side.*)

Have you come, Raghunath and Sadashib! See, Kalapahad is not willing to openly take part in the war. His intention is not known. I see that I shall not rely on him. We have to manage with the soldiers he has given to us. Raghunath, you will move the soldiers on the west where the Army Chief of Mukunda Deb is stationed. Sadashib, you will be on the eastern side to counter Dhanurdhar Baliarsingh. You may not attack. Only keep watch. I shall be in the front because Mukunda Deb always leads from the front. There is maximum danger in the middle. I consider that it will be right for me to be in the middle.

RAGHU : Right, Maharaj. Yet, we have little hope of wining in the war. Mukunda Deb is determined to fight like a solid rock. He is calling this war with us as treachery, selfishness, but he has forgotten how selfish he is. The sacred throne of Utkal is not for a common employee. The throne may remain vacant if there is no royal progeny. How can a servant sit on it? There lies the blunder.

SADA : There was only one suggestion to Maharaj – please get ready to accept the throne.

	Well, Maharaj is not a beggar so that he will get the throne as a gift from Mukunda Deb. Next, he has adorned the throne as the king. Oh dear, you have committed a blunder. Why do you show it off? Accept your blunder and give way.
RAMA	: No, that won't happen, Sadashib. Now he has resolved to make war. He has a vast army and he will fight. We are poor, negligible, and without strength. We may sacrifice our lives in the war. Yet, how can we accept injustice knowingly?
RAGHU	: No, Maharaj! We will sacrifice our lives but we will not overlook injustice. Nawab of Banga has sent some Muslim soldiers. Kalapahad has also sent some soldiers, perhaps five thousand.
SADA	: The rest belongs to Sarang Garh. Of course, it is meagre. Yet, we have to fight.
RAMA	: We need not fear, Sadashib. Victory is always on the side of righteousness, justice, and truth. We may have nothing but we have truth on our side, justice as our vow. We are not to be quite hopeless. Savitri could save her husband Satyaban from Lord Yama by dint of her virtue. Virtue is our strength, truth is our saviour, the Lord of the Universe is our last refuge. Come, Raghunath and Sadashib, you need not fear. We have to get ready.

(*Curtain*)

SCENE VI
The Battlefield.
(Mukunda Deb, Dhanurdhar, Army Chief and Minister are standing.)

MINISTER : This war has no end, Maharaj. There is still war even if they are defeated again and again. War for Ramachandra Bhanja is his food and sleep and daily work. So much of bloodshed is in vain. He was imprisoned that day. He should not have been released, Maharaj. Today, go and imprison him, Chief. There is no more respite. It is good for us. Our first duty is to save the state, Maharaj.

MUKUNDA : No, Minister. It might be your mistake but not ours. It's not uprightness not to reprieve the prisoner when he begs for life. It's not righteousness on our part. Righteousness is our first priority. State, and peace follow next and finally, happiness and enjoyment. Ramachandra Bhanja may be our fierce enemy. But, what then is our duty when he begs for his freedom in the name of righteousness, and truth?

DHANU : Right, Maharaj.

CHIEF : Then, will it continue like this?

MUKUNDA : No, Commander, when we realise that Ramachandra Bhanja is not trustworthy, you may then imprison him, or kill him as a traitor to the state and Dharma, but not before that. Man may err once or twice.

CHIEF : He may be forgiven once or twice,

		Maharaj. Assuming that I ignore the previous occasions. What about the treacherous scheme of murdering you in the battle field. Fortunately, the Nawab of Banga arrived at the nick of time. How can a person be pardonable after such betrayal? Yet, I freed him on the orders of the Maharaj.
MUKUNDA	:	If necessary, Chief, you have to free him again on the orders of the same Maharaj.
MINISTER	:	No, Maharaj, we will not carry out such orders again.
MUKUNDA	:	No, Minister, there is no chance of such orders. Why do you think of defying the orders? You may imprison Ramachandra Bhanja today. Chief, please proceed to the battle field. May Baliarsingh too join you! Kalapahad has sent a new batch of soldiers. You may have to exert special efforts. Minister, please return to the fort. I'll wait for the arrival of soldiers.

(*All except Mukunda Deb exit.*)

In fact, there is no end to this war. It has to be finished today. You are committing a blunder, Ramachandra. There is a limit to forgiving you. But no more. Try to be worthy of pardon, otherwise you will be punished. I am not Mukunda only, but Mukunda Deb, the king of this state. I should look after the wellbeing of the kingdom. I should take care of the peace and happiness of the subjects; or else it will be the negligence of duty to the state.

(*Bugle sound of the soldiers comes from a distance.*)

The soldiers are coming. This war bugle sounds sweetly. It creates life in the lifeless body.

(*Soldiers enter.*)

SOLDIERS : Victory to Maharaj.

MUKUNDA : Soldiers, this war has continued for a long time unnecessarily. I have needlessly caused you a lot of suffering and unhappiness. I have put the citizens in peril. We have to do something about it. It should not continue as it has continued so far. You have today appeared in the battle field. The glory, prosperity, good fortune depends on you now. You have to win this battle today. Still, you are not at peace. The bitterest enemy of the kingdom is inside it. You are fighting your brother today. This not a real war. You have to face the vast and valiant army of the Muslims tomorrow. You have to show in that war how Odias may sacrifice their life, but shall not surrender a needle point space to the enemy. If you win that war, you can keep the honour, name and fame intact, otherwise, shame, humiliation, and defeat will stare at your face. Let's go now, soldiers. Shout victory chants. Blow on the war bugles.

SOLDIERS : Victory to Maharaj!

(*Blowing of the bugles, and soldiers exit.*)

MUKUNDA : Excellent war music. Minister has returned

to the fort. Chief and Baliarsingh have taken their positions in the battle field. An early farewell! What might be the outcome of today's battle? Ramachandra Bhanja, I now feel what I have not felt for you so long - hatred. What did you do though you are being born in a palace? How can you do so much harm to the state, to your own race? Fie on you, Ramachandra Bhanja! (*finds Ramachandra Bhanja approaching him.*) Here is Ramachandra Bhanja, appearing before the enemy holding a flag of truce. Still I am generous. You have correctly recognised your enemy, Ramachandra. You are quite handsome and graceful, but the sign of terror in your face always frightens me. Even in the battle field today I am petrified. No. No.
(*Ramachandra Bhanja enters.*)
Is it the proposal for truce, O King?

RAMA : You have rightly understood, Maharaj. Proposal for truce it is. Proposal for truce is the need of the state at this hour. Proposal should be offered at the time of need. (*secretly draws out his sword.*) Only the proposal will not do. (*attacks Mukunda Deb.*) Now sit on the throne of Odisha for good, stupid. (*Exit.*)

MUKUNDA : (*collapses*) You have to kill me with your own hands, Oh Ramachandra. Oh! Why didn't you kill me completely?
(*Suleman along with Minister enter from the opposite direction.*)

MINISTER	:	Horrible! Horrible! Horrible! What a deed! What a horrible deed!
SULEMAN	:	Absolute ruin! What is it, Dear Minister?
MUKUNDA	:	Who? Minister? Have you come back?
MINISTER	:	I have come back, Maharaj. What can I do?
MUKUNDA	:	Bye! No more! This is my last. Isn't the Chief here? Oh, isn't Baliarsingh here? Farewell. Bid me farewell, Minister. Badshah! Badshah! Farewell. How can I repay the debt of your love at the final hour of death? Farewell. Farewell. Farewell. Oh, my heart is failing. The wind of life is getting colder. Oh! My throat is choking. Farewell, Minister. Farewell, Badshah. Farewell, Mother Utkal. Farewell. (*Dies*.)
MINISTER	:	All hopes have almost come to an end with this, Badshah. All conjectures are final. You have beholden the brilliant prosperity of Utkal. You will now see, Badshah, her downfall. It all came to naught in a moment. I could see all these as I returned with you. Ah! Why did I come back? Just to see this misfortune.
SULEMAN	:	Ah! The resplendent jewel of this vast Utkal! How mean is the weapon of an assassin! How ugly! How critical! We met each other in this battle field. That was a day in life and this is another. We see off each other in another battle field. Farewell. Maharaj. Suleman has seen a lot of Hindus. He has killed several Hindus with his own sword. But I have seen only

one Hindu like you. Muslims admit defeat before you in the battle field. Still, there is glory in that defeat. Farewell, Maharaj. Mukunda, the brilliant jewel of holy Utkal! He is now lying on dust, Minister. My heart is torn to pieces. What kind of work you were born to do, oh, Muslim General Kalapahad! You are already deprived of your religion, caste, and the honour of your clan. You have in the long run done this heinous deed with the help of an assassin.

(*Curtain*)

ACT 4
SCENE I
The Royal Court of Ramachandra Bhanja.

(*Ramachandra Bhanja, Raghunath and Sadashib are seated. A dancer is standing.*)

DANCER: (Song)
Come, let's joyfully sing this sweet night
To the tune of flute that dispels all grief.
The moon rises in the new moon sky,
The night glows with sweet silvery light,
As if to shower love on earth and sky.
In the nectar sweet moonlit night
Lily dances playfully in the Chudang pond
Sweet murmur rises in the Bhargavi water,
Hills and dales, houses and vacant fields,
Are all enchanted with nectar effect. (*Exit.*)

RAMA : Are you asking me, Sadashib? I can do that now. But I don't feel like doing it. I don't feel fine.

SADA : Will it do even if you don't feel like, Maharaj? You have to sit only in Barabati; or else why this pointless bloodshed? You have to sit. Sage Agastya was doing meditation under the tree to be Lord Indra. When his meditation was complete, he adorned the throne of Indra in the heaven.

RAGHU : When Shishunag reigned Magadha, he sat on the throne of Magadha.

SADA : Nanda also occupied the throne after Maha Nanda.

RAMA : Chandragupta defeated the last Nanda ruler and he didn't stay in his house but adorned the throne.

SADA : Maharaj Gupta also did the same thing.

RAGHU : Yayati Keshari too got hold of Odisha during Indra Deba's reign and ruled from the throne.

SADA : Chudanga Deb defeated Subarna Keshari and also adorned his throne. This is the go of the world. Who will enjoy the fruits of victory if the victor doesn't?

RAGHU : It's true. It was just recently, Gobinda Vidyadhar ...

RAGHU : Gobinda Vidyadhar! Whose name did you utter, Raghunath? He surreptitiously killed all the princes and became the king, not defeating them in war. No. similarly Babur, whose grandson Akbar is the Mughal Emperor, also defeated King Ibrahim and killed him to occupy the throne of Delhi.

RAGHU : Similarly, Maharaj, you will adorn the

RAMA	:

golden throne at Barabati Fort. We have to make all necessary arrangements for it. If necessary, we will fight.

RAMA : It's true, Raghunath. But it's very painful. Even after Mukunda Deb died, I didn't know what his fault was. All of you offered him the throne. Oh, the man died at once. It's not in the horoscope of the king of Saranga Garh to make his fortune out of somebody's death. It's very painful. But what is the way out? That's the battle field. All are equal before it whether he is the king or a subject, a criminal or the innocent. But, sorrow does not know logic, Sadashib. It occurs when it should. You or I cannot arrest it. You may go, if you like. We shall decide it later. I feel depressed now. I'll have some rest.

SADA : So, we beg your leave, Maharaj.

(*Sadashib and Raghunath exit.*)

RAMA : Rest? There is no rest in this life as long as the goal is not accomplished. One obstacle was Mukunda Deb; he is finished. But the present thorn is an invited one. On the one hand, it is easy to get rid of, it is very difficult on the other. Even then, the goal is fixed from the beginning. Determination is firm. Duty is definite. Duty! There are two duties before me now. The first is to enter Barabati and the second is to destroy Kalapahad. Both the jobs are very important but very difficult too. Still, not impossible. Of course, we won't get

Kalapahad's help in occupying Barabati. To garner the help of the denizens of Barabati to destroy Kalpahad– it is not also impossible. I'll try it first. Kalapahad is not the enemy of Saranga Garh now. He is the enemy of entire Odisha. It's easy then. Minister will agree with me in that case. What is impossible if I can win the Army Chief and Baliarsingh to my side? Then, Barabati can be won without any efforts. At first, I have to concentrate on Kalapahad. Mukunda Deb belonged to our clan, our religion and state. That love and affection is absent from Kalapahad. What cannot be achieved by means of war can be achieved through cleverness. War is a delusion, a means to use cleverness.
(*A messenger enters.*)
Who is there?

MESS : Maharaj, I am the messenger from Bhubaneswar. You are the Gajapati of Odisha now. It's too unbearable for us. It's a great torture on religion. There is not a single temple left in Ekamra forest which has not been smashed by Kalapahad's club. Please, take some preventive measures, Maharaj. It's intolerable. We shiver to behold it. Blood boils in us. Are Odias so demoralised, Maharaj?

RAMA : No. Odisha was in anarchy for some days. Kalapahad was playing havoc. It's over. The ruler of Odisha is not weak any longer. Kalapahad? If a number of Odia soldiers are set against you, they will be invincible. If you think of your wellbeing, go back to your own country immediately. Don't worry, Messenger. Kalapahad will recompense for what destruction he has wrought before he leaves for his state. Our state will be henceforth properly governed. The subjects will be in happiness and prosperity. Religion will be free of enemies.

(*Curtain*)

SCENE II

A road in the fields.

(*Dhanurdhar Baliarsingh, Gobinda and Gopal enter.*)

DHANU	:	Gopal, you had a big stroke of a sword on your back, didn't you?
GOPAL	:	Yes, I had. It's getting well.
DHANU	:	What about your waist, Gobinda?
GOBINDA	:	It's not better. It might be well soon.
DHANU	:	You suffered a lot for the kingdom, dear. Sons have to suffer like this for the kingdom, for the motherland. They have to give up food and sleep. They have to sacrifice their joys and happiness. They have to bleed profusely, otherwise how can the motherland be safe? Bloodshed! Bloodshed! Maharaj has shed his blood for the motherland. You have to do like that, dear.

GOBINDA & GOPAL	:	We will.

(Minister and Army Chief enter.)

DHANU	:	Have you come, esteemed Minister? Have you come, esteemed Army Chief? How long shall we protect the fort of Barabati? This vast state of Odisha is now contracted to the territory of Cuttack. Beyond this city Ramachandra Bhanja is the king. Beyond that, Kalapahad is the king. There is anarchy in the kingdom. It shall not continue like this any longer, esteemed Minister. To save the fort is not our only duty. Our duty is more significant, more vast. It concerns all Odisha. It's now all over. Why brooding? Save the fort, save the capital. Bid me farewell. I have a few soldiers left with me. Let me move around the fort once. I'll check how powerful the traitor is; how brilliant the enemy of Dharma is. What more is left in this life, esteemed Minister? What is there in joy or sorrow? What should I live for? Why should I have any attachment with life? But before I die I shall once create an upheaval in the state. I shall set fire to the forests and hills once more. I'll set deluge in the rivers and seas once. I'll paint the comely face of the motherland with blackness. Dear Chief, I started my life in the battle field, in the destructive storm that swept the battle field, amidst the sounds of weapons, having listened

	to the pathetic cries of the dying, having drenched myself in human blood from head to foot. Let me leave now. Protect the fort. Save the capital. We shall meet when I return. Otherwise it's our last meeting. Bid me farewell, Minister. Bid me farewell, Chief. Gobinda and Gopal, Come with me. (*Dhanurdhar Baliarsingh, Gobinda and Gopal exit.*)
CHIEF	: The old man departed. What brilliance, esteemed Minister! He seems like a streak of lightening, a violent earthquake, a fierce wild fire. He disappeared like these. What is the need of meeting again, Chief, if we can't save the state from the enemy? What is the need of exchange of words? No, esteemed Minister, we shall lay down our lives to keep up the glory of the motherland. (*Raghunath enters.*)
MINISTER	: All right, Chief. Are you Raghunath Bhanja? The son of Ramachandra Bhanja's brother?
RAGHU	: No, esteemed Minister, I am his distant cousin. Now a courtier.
MINISTER	: What brings you here?
RAGHU	: The ruler of Sarang Garh has understood that Kalapahad is an enemy of Odisha. Presently, the enemy has to be driven out of the state.
CHIEF	: Then, he has understood it.
RAGHU	: My errand is – the king is trying to fight

	Kalapahad together with you. Mukunda Deb was the enemy of Ramachandra Bhanja. The state of Odisha is not his enemy. Presently, every citizen should fight with all their souls to save the state. You should all forget the old enmity. Please, assist the king of Sarang Garh. He is determined to fight Kalapahad and keep the glory of Odisha intact by driving him out.
MINISTER	: It's Ramachandra Bhanja's duty at present, Raghunath Bhanja. It's fine that he will do it. We will assist him. What else? We will fight to save the state as he will do. It is what will be our assistance to him. What more help? Raghunath Bhanja, please convey that we are pleased with this wish of the king of Sarang Garh.
RAGHU	: Help us with soldiers.
CHIEF	: If need arises.
RAGHU	: Then, I shall convey the message. Let me beg your leave now.
MINISTER	: May you leave, Raghunath Bhanja! We will help. (*Raghunath exits.*) At this time of adversity, we should not have enmity with two people. Ramachandra Bhanja is not now the enemy of the state. If necessary we will have to forget all enmity and place him on the throne. Our first duty is to save the state. Hence, we have to tackle Kalapahad first. As long as he is not driven out of the country, Kalapahad cannot be believed.

CHIEF	:	One thing, esteemed Minister, everything is possible. We may support Ramachandra Bhanja with soldiers, with money, but he should not be allowed to enter the capital as long as Kalapahad is in our state. Then other considerations arise.
MINISTER	:	You are right. However, we have to ensure that Ramachandra Bhanja is under our control. Who knows what He wills! Come, esteemed Minister, we shall have a look around the fort. It is our duty now to protect the fort. Dhanurdhar Baliarsingh has left us. He threw himself into the hands of the enemy. He has rightly said, "What is attachment with life?" Come, Chief, he has done what he has understood as his duty. We shall perform our duty.

(*Curtain*)

SCENE III
The Chamber of Kalapahad.
(*Kalapahad and Dillir are seated.*)

KALA	:	Please tell, Dillir Khan, the General is not in Odisha.
DILLIR	:	Badshah may ask, "Where is he then?"
KALA	:	He has returned to the kingdom and is camping on the bank of the Ganga. No. I shall go back soon. As soon as possible. Might be in fifteen days, Dillir. Whatever you may say is not untrue. But you will speak the truth in advance. This kind of truth one day Mohammad said while he was fleeing from Mecca to Medina. I

		mean, when an enemy asked him, "Where is Mohammad?", Mohammad said that Mohammad might be in Medina. Did he not speak the truth in advance, Dillir?
DILLIR	:	Yes, of course. He was Mohammad, your Excellency. I am a mere Dillir Khan.
KALA	:	Look, a little future truth may be said for any noble cause. Similarly, in Hindu religion, Yudhishthira had said, "Whether human or elephant, Ashwatthama is killed"
DILLIR	:	No, Your Highness, I cannot do it. Please excuse me.
KALA	:	Can't you?
DILLIR	:	No, I cannot.
KALA	:	Then you will be in prison as long as I have not returned.
DILLIR	:	I don't mind, Mr. General. But I will not tell a lie.
KALA	:	Who is there? (*Background voice : "Your Highness." Four soldiers enter.*) Put him in chains, soldiers. (*Soldiers put Dillir Khan in chains.*) Go Dillir, enjoy the fruits of your action.
DILLIR	:	I don't care, General. (*Soldiers lead him away.*)
KALA	:	This Dillir, no, why only Dillir? All Muslims are stupid. Hindus too are foolish. But if Hindus change into Muslims or Muslims convert into Hindus, they are not like that. This second category may be clever. They must be gaining some knowledge while

courting another religion. Of course, they win some righteousness. I have now gained a lot of merit. I enjoy a lot of pleasure in breaking down Hindu temples and idols. How glorious! I will make this state devoid of temples and idols. I will convert Puri into Mecca. One more thing before that. To be the king. No, this is not the goal of my life. My goal is to win kingdoms and spread religion. I shall win this state by means my prowess. I don't mind who becomes the king. That stupid Ramachandra Bhanja might be the king. But I'll make him my slave first. I will make him a slave of the Muslim victor. I will occupy Barabati Fort by dint of physical force and cleverness. I'll avenge my humiliation from Mukunda Deb. It is my first duty. I have not come for the welfare of this state. Only to accomplish my goal. How do I bother what happens after that? You are in delusion, oh, the Nawab of Banga. How do you think that Kalapahad will go back on your orders? Eh!

(*Curtain*)

SCENE IV
The path in the garden.
(*Leelabati enters.*)

LEELA : (SONG)
Oh, the moon! Oh, the stars!
Why do you rise in sky?
Your invisible nectary touch
Make the lily die.
She is pale in sorrow,
bows down in grief
Can it open its tender eyes
To have a look at you?
Oh, the bright sun, come down soon
In the water of the pond, burn her down
Never ever disappoint her,
This sorrow is too much for her to bear

Oh, Ushayinee! Ushayinee! It's because of my one blunder, one betrayal! Of course, Mukunda Deb is not immortal. He wouldn't have sat on the throne for ever. That's true. Who is immortal on this earth? Who enjoys perpetual happiness? Therefore, it is not my job to bring an end to everybody's life. It's is a big sin, great impiousness, injustice and treachery, isn't it? I have committed homicide and regicide. I have caused anarchy to Utkal. I have poisoned the faith in me. I have prepared a beautiful garland of flowers and hid in it a   poisonous snake and placed it on your neck, Ushayini, so that the serpent would come out and sting you. So, has it been done. The state will

now pass into the hands of the Muslims. I have done it. The people of the state will be dipped in blemish. I have done it. I wrote to you with love and you sent the soldiers, Oh Queen. Ah! Let my life be torn into two! On the one hand, I repent for my vice and on the other hand, there is my devotion to my husband. Devotion for husband! Still, he is the deity of my life to be worshipped. O the Lord of my Life, you have done injustice. You have surrendered the kingdom to the enemy. Yes, you have done that, haven't you? Even then I am your consort. I have half the share of your sin. No, dear, I shall not desert you. Oh, in the name of God, carry me with you in both happiness and sorrow, virtue and vice.
(*Ramachandra Bhanja enters.*)
Have you come, My Lord?

RAMA : I have come.
LEELA : Don't drive me away from you, My Lord. Take me with you. I am a woman, frail, and poor. Yet, I am not so wretched and weak. I am the partner of your life, your companion for ever.
RAMA : I am as such, Leelabati.
LEELA : Dear husband, it seems that between you and me, there is a distance of seven seas, like the sky is from the Netherlands, like the Meru top from us. Oh, the Lord of my life, what makes you so worried. Your eyes are pale. Your face has lost its

	radiance. Smile has faded from your lips. Reveal everything to me, dear. My heart is throbbing. My life seems poisonous to me. I shall get rid of a half of your burden. Pray, tell me.
RAMA	: Burden on my life, Queen! There is nothing like that with me. One burden is that there is the Muslim enemy in our kingdom. We have to drive them out.
LEELA	: You must, dear. You must drive the enemy from the state. It would have been better if you had done it from the beginning. You have made that mistake. You have helped Kalapahad first to fight Mukunda Deb. Mukunda Deb lost his life in that battle. There is anarchy in the state now. There is little hope left for the wellbeing of the state. Muslims are the bitter enemies of our state. Drive them first, dear. I am a woman. It's not my duty to appear on the battle field. Even then I am your wife and you are my husband. Husband is the Lord of the wife. Go, dear.Face the Muslims in the battle field and save the state.
RAMA	: I shall go, Leelabati. It is now the duty of my life. I shall go. Return to the palace. Why are you remaining awake unnecessarily? Go back. I too shall go. There is no leisure. (Exit.)
LEELA	: You'll drive Kalapahad away. All right, My Lord. The state will be in peace and happiness. Still, the burden on my life does not disappear. It is a grave sin. Ushayinee!

Ushayinee! Everything will be restored. The king will sit on the throne. Welfare and glory of the state will be restored. How can you get back your darling? A grave sin! How can I be relieved of this sin? Impossible! Impossible! Impossible! (*Curtain*)

SCENE V
The camp of Kalapahad.
(*Dhanurdhar Baliarsingh is seated. Dillir Khan is in chains.*)

DHANU : We, Odias, are not against any religion, Dillir Khan. We have set up Jagannath Dham at Neelachal so that all the races and clans of the world can be united. We have always embraced all the infidels and aliens. We have allowed Muslim devotee Haridas to sit on our lap. We have placed a tooth of Lord Buddha in the idol of Lord Jagannath and worship it as God. We are not against any religion, Dillir Khan. We are against the enemy of our state only. Whenever he has stood as our enemy, we have smashed his arrogance. Whenever he has begged refuge from us, whether he is a Muslim, or a Hindu or any alien, we are giving them asylum.

DILLIR : I know it, General. You need not tell me that the Odias are generous. I have seen it with my own eyes. I have seen that they are as heroic in the battle field as they are courteous in conversation. I have felt that they are as liberal in dealings as they are

		noble in forgiving enemies. Therefore, I am a devotee of Odias as Haridas and Salabega were.
DHANU	:	I shall discharge my duties now, Dillir Khan. You have been imprisoned by Kalapahad. I'll set you free.
DILLIR	:	I am a subject of Banga. The General of the vast Banga army is imprisoned by you. How can I be freely returning to my country, while our General is in chains and in slavery? It's impossible, General. I shall stay with him in chains, and in slavery. If I am to die, I shall die with him. I beg your excuse, General. I am grateful to you for your kindness. But I am unable to accept your offer.
DHANU	:	Odias are generous about Dharma, Dillir Khan, but he turns ferocious when he sees that their generosity is violated. Your General has destroyed holy temples of our state, smashed the idols, and defied religion. Therefore, the people of Utkal are furious. Now he is the enemy of our state. If he is set free, it will be ominous for the state, Dillir Khan.
DILLIR	:	It may be so, General. I don't mean that. How can I urge you to set the enemy of your state free?
DHANU	:	No, Dillir Khan, Odias are never afraid of their enemies. We may be vanquished, oppressed, and destitute, yet we are not narrow-minded and we never take recourse to meanness. Dillir Khan you

	are generous and noble. We don't offend the race in which there are people like you. (*Releasing him*) You may leave, Dillir Khan. I will set your General free. If he creates disturbance in the state, he will be suitably punished by the Odias. Gobinda and Gopal, bring the Muslim General here. I shall set him free – no, you will yourself set him free with your own hands, Dillir Khan. (*Gobinda and Gopal escort Kalapahad.*) Set him free, Dillir Khan.
DILLIR	: (*Releasing Kalapahad.*) The generous race of Odias are setting you free now, General of Banga.
DHANU	: Farewell, General. Farewell, Dillir Khan. I hear the call of duty elsewhere. Let me go. Come Gobinda and Gopal. (*Exit with Gobinda and Gopal.*)
DILLIR	: Odias are very generous, Mr. General. It is a great sin to be the enemy of this race. It's the order of the Badshah that we shall go back to our state, Your Highness.
KALA	: You are right, Dillir Khan. But I didn't beg for freedom. I feel that as if I am free on my own merit. Because, I can set myself free on my own.
DILLIR	: I have myself set you free now. Come, I request you to return to our own state.
KALA	: I spurn your request, Dillir Khan. I may be cruel, stubborn, and indomitable, but never a beggar. I don't bow my head before my enemy as a jackal does before a lion. You are free. Go back to the state

		happily. Keep it in mind, Dillir Khan, I won't do that.
DILLIR	:	Then you may stay here. I cannot stay in this kingdom any longer. *(Exit.)*
KALA	:	Well Dhanurdhar Baliarsingh has imprisoned me twice and set me free twice. I shall imprison that Odia ten times and set him free ten times. I don't want any kingdom. I have given up that desire. Now my only goal is victory, revenge and spread of religion. Dillir, convey it to Badshah. I must have vanquished Odisha before that. No more delay. Hurry up!

(Curtain)

SCENE VI
The camp of Ramachandra Bhanja.

(Ramachandra Bhanja along with Sadashib enters.)

RAMA	:	I admit that Raghunath is a great warrior and generous too. But he is not skillful. He has no knowledge of politics. He has no consideration for duty or otherwise.
SADA	:	You are right, Maharaj. Raghunath is incompetent in these matters.
RAMA	:	Therefore, I say that you can do it. You can very well do it. But keep it a secret from Raghunath because he is unable to decide between what is good and what is bad. He cannot distinguish between what is to be kept a secret and what is to be revealed.
SADA	:	It's true, Maharaj.

RAMA	:	Do you know that I had sent a message to Dhanurdhar Baliarsingh to negotiate friendship with the Minister of Mukunda Deb? But he has not accepted it. He had imprisoned Kalapahad. He did the right thing. These men are the glory of the state. He himself set him free. He has now targeted Saranga Garh. I hear that he is coming like a hurricane. We have to obstruct that whirlwind, Sadashib.
SADA	:	Certainly, Maharaj. But Raghunath's help is necessary in this regard.
RAMA	:	No. In face to face encounter this whirlwind cannot be obstructed, Sadashib. Therefore, I say 'skill' which Raghunath doesn't have. You alone can do it. No one else in this state can do it.
SADA	:	What can I do Maharaj?
RAMA	:	Dhanurdhar is coming at a tremendous speed. There are only two soldiers with him. The rest are following him. So, kill him before the battle. We presented ourselves humbly before the enemy, made truce with the enemy but he is so aggressive, so beastly that he does not accept us. Why this futile bloodshed? Why this wastage of money? We have to accomplish our goal with ease. Can you do it, Sadashib? After all, you will be the king of Sarang Garh when I shall adorn the throne of Odisha.
SADA	:	Yes, I can do it, Maharaj.
RAMA	:	But in a clandestine way. If Raghunath

	knows, tell him it's war. You see that it is dangerous. Maintain complete secrecy. Keep the things to your heart.
SADA	: I will, Maharaj.
RAMA	: All right, then. There is a limit to arrogance, an end to aggression. (*Background Voice.*) Come, Gobinda and Gopal.
RAMA	: What is this noise? Who is being called? (*Dhanurdhar enters.*) Oh, Dhanurdhar Baliarsingh. Look, Sadashib. (*Exit.*)
SADA	: (*Attacks Dhanurdhar*) All right. The price of the throne of Sarang Garh is so small! (*Exit.*)
DHANU	: (*falling down*) Oh, what a blow! Gobinda! Gopal! (*Gobinda and Gopal enter.*)
GOBINDA	: What is this, Gopal?
DHANU	: Have you come, Gopal? Maharaj is calling me.
GOPAL.	No. No one is calling you. Where? What has happened?
DHANU	: Can't you hear, Gopal? He is calling me. Prataprudra Deb is sitting. Mukunda Deb is sitting. I'm coming, Maharaj. I saw you after a long time. My eyes are consecrated. I have got the jewel of my heart. Oh! How fortunate I am! What are you saying, Maharaj? Is there more work left yet? Yes, shall I do it? I, Dhanurdhar Baliarsingh? No. Not I? Then I am going.

Gobinda and Gopal, tell the Minister and the Army Chief that Maharaj called me and I am going. I'm coming, Maharaj. One word more. Stay, Gobinda and Gopal, you suffered a lot. I'm coming, Maharaj. One more word. My country! My country! My country! Oh, God! (*dies.*)
(*Curtain*)

ACT V
SCENE I
The Chamber of Ramachandra Bhanja.
(*Ramachandra Bhanja is seated*)

RAMA : There are two enemies to my goal. Both of them are weaker than before. Dhanurdhar is gone. It means that half the hurdle on the path of occupying Barabati fort is gone. Sadashib finally proved to be a nice weapon. Again, a half of Kalapahad's army has been destroyed by Dhanurdhar. Yet, the rest are also not small. If I get the chance, I can be very capable. Is it possible? Who knows? Kalapahad is not an open enemy, but a friend. Minister has rightly understood. "We will be friends. We will help you with soldiers. We will do whatever is needed but we'll not allow you to enter Barabati." What friendship! I did not adopt these means to share love with you, Minister. I have to do it by any means – either by intrigue, or force or cleverness. My soul is in Barabati. Life is

	meaningless without it. Barabati is on one end of the scale; my life is on the other. I see that the first end is going down. So, life is useless. No. By all means. (*Sadashib enters.*) Have you come, Sadashib?
SADA	: Yes, Maharaj. What is the progress? It's getting delayed. We must do something soon.
RAMA	: I see Sadashib that you are more concerned than me. Have patience. Slow and steady wins the race. All will be settled by and by.
SADA	: A lot of time has passed, Maharaj, since the death of Dhanurdhar Baliarsingh. Every passing day seems a decade to me.
RAMA	: Every passing day appears less than a day, Sadashib. (*Raghunath enters.*)
RAGHU	: I hear that Kalapahad is coming. Muslim soldiers are very large in number. People on my way were saying, "Kalapahad is passing."
RAMA	: Kalapahad! There is no reason for his sudden arrival. There is only a proposal for war. There has been no declaration yet. Is he already prepared for that? Who knows? Still, get the army ready. (*Hue and cry comes closer.*) What is this noise about? Is Kalapahad so near? (*Kalapahad enters with soldiers.*) Welcome, oh, General of Banga.
KALA	: There is no need for invitation, King. I see,

		the occupation of Barabati will start from here. So, I don't wait for any invitaion. Get ready, Ramachandra Bhanja. Don't be afraid. I shall not kill you. Only imprisonment.
SADA	:	Let's go away, Maharaj. Oh, My God! (*Exit.*)
RAMA	:	No, General.
KALA	:	No more delay. Soldiers!
RAGHU	:	No, Kalapahad, you are making a mistake. If you try to imprison even a child of Saranga Garh, you have to fight. What to speak of the King!
RAMA	:	Please consider, you will surely get your share, General as agreed earlier. Wherefore this battle?
RAGHU	:	There is no question of agreement, Maharaj. Only war. Odia knows only war; no agreement. Come, Kalapahad.
KALA	:	All right. See for yourself. Mahib Khan! (*There is a duel between Raghunath and Mahib Khan. Both of them exit. A number of Muslim soldiers follow them.*) Well, it's war. Do you see, Ramachandra Bhanja? Come, don't delay.
RAMA	:	Why war? Your share is all right.
KALA	:	I am not a beggar. I am the victor.
RAMA	:	You will get the benefit of victory, General. What more do you want?
KALA	:	I'll certainly get it. But not because of anybody's favour but by dint of my prowess.
RAMA	:	Then, what is your wish, General? Be clear.

KALA	:	To imprison you.
RAMA	:	There is no need of negotiation. I am not well. Wait, General, let me go. (*attempting to go away.*)
KALA	:	Halt, Ramachandra Bhanja. Arrest him, soldiers. (*Soldiers put him in chains.*)
RAMA	:	You have power, General. You have arrested me, but listen to one thing. Listen to me.
KALA	:	You may tell a hundred things. Why one thing, Ramachandra Bhanja?
RAMA	:	No, only one thing. You want to possess Barabati. Do it. You want to be the king of this state. Do it. But make me free. Not for the whole life. But only for a day. Only for once. My dream of Barabati will be ruined. No, make me free for one day. Now I am a prisoner! Alas! My destiny!
KALA	:	Lead him away, soldiers. (*Exit.*)
SOLDIER	:	Come.
RAMA	:	Where shall I go? Oh, only one day! How fierce! Prisoner! No. No. No.
SOLDIER	:	Come. (*Soldiers exit with the prisoner.*) (*Raghunath enters from the opposite direction.*)
RAGHU	:	There is no one here. Why? I penetrated through the ranks of Muslim soldiers with the help of this sword just to release the king. But in vain. Today, the king of Saranga Garh is imprisoned. Tomorrow, the Muslims will attack Barabati. It's a great

blunder in life. Now, I should be careful. We have to keep up the glory of the state. We have to protect the fort from the enemies. Then the release of Ramachandra Bhanja; Or else, it's a great deluge. All the kings and the subjects will be submerged in it. It's a great blunder, King. We have to take leave from the world after handing over the holy land of Utkal to the enemies. (*Curtain*)

SCENE II
The Battlefield.

(*The Army Chief of Mukunda Deb along with soldiers enter.*)

SOLDIER : (SONG)
In the battle today, we'll kill the enemy
Or else never shall we come back
We'll sacrifice our life in battle field
Flooding it with their brothers' blood.

Come brothers, come
Life has no meaning
If we can't kill the enemy,
To earn name and fame.

Let's relieve mother's sorrow
Piercing the enemies' chests
We left behind children and wife
Giving up our love for life.

CHIEF : Oh, Mother Utkal. Today is a day of trial for your destiny. If this is the last test, you can be fortunate enough to enjoy heavenly joys or else, you will be a poor beggar of the streets. All your treasures are finished; only your glory is left. Keep up your glory yourself, Mother. This holy Mahanadi is flowing down for ever as the blue mountain Kapilas is standing erect projecting its beautiful peak into the sky on this heroic land. This river will not flow as usual like this. This mountain will not project its peak as usual. Can an Odia see this with his own eyes? My heart is broken to pieces, Mother.

(*Raghunath along with soldiers enters.*)

ALL : Sing.
(Song)
Let's relieve mother's sorrow
Piercing the enemies' chests
We left behind children and wife
Giving up our love for life. (E*xit.*)

CHIEF : Let's not delay, Soldiers. We have to sacrifice our lives today, drench the battlefield with our blood, and dip the bosom of our motherland with our blood. You have built up this state with your life. You have stood in many alien battle fields, pierced the chests of the enemies with your swords, won many laurels of victory. You are the same warriors of Mother Utkal. Come. Let's not delay. We hear the call of Mother Utkal. It seems as if Goddess Durga seated on the lion's back

	is roaring. Come, soldiers. Raghunath Bhanja has come. Welcome. It's a critical time of test. (E*xit*.)
	(*Kalapahad enters with soldiers.*)
SOLDIERS	: Victory to Allah!
KALA	: Look, soldiers, swear that you will not return to your camps as long as a single Odia soldier is left in the battle field.
SOLDIERS	: We swear.
KALA	: Trample the enemy.
SOLDIERS	: We will.
KALA	: Drink the blood of the enemies.
SOLDIERS	: We will.
KALA	: Then you will retreat.
SOLDIERS	: We will.
KALA	: Do you remember, soldiers, when you hear the signal turn back immediately and flee?
SOLDIERS	: We will.
KALA	: But be careful. Very careful. When they become exhausted by chasing you, make an about turn immediately.
SOLDIERS	: We will.
KALA	: And attack them
SOLDIERS	: We will.
KALA	: Victory is doubtful in frontal attack. Odias fight with dedication. These Odias are very fierce and stupid as well. They may die but not accept defeat. They won't even retreat.
SOLDIER	: They may die but not accept defeat! Are they sheep?
KALA	: Victory is certain, *soldiers*.

(There is too much noise and sounds of clashing weapons from the background.)
The sounds of clashing weapons! The enemy then is very near. Get ready.
(Odia soldiers enter. They had a face to face fight with Muslim soldiers. Kalapahad and his soldiers flee and they are chased by the Odia soldiers. Banambar and Sadashib enter from the opposite direction.)

BANA : This Kalapahad, - his cleverness is as good as his name, brother Sadashib.

SADA : Yes, very clever and skillful too. See, what he did that day. Oh, my God! I fled. Had I been there, I would not have survived.

BANA : You are not less clever, brother. You disappeared all on a sudden like a dog fleeing from the tiger during the hunt. Is it not a clever deed? If others die, there is flood but if we die, there is deluge.

SADA : Only Raghunath is left. He must have been beaten black and blue. His back must have been sore. It seemed as if palm fruits were falling one after another.
(There is much noise and sounds of clashing weapons from the background.)
Eh, they are fast approaching. Oh, my God! Hide, hide. Where is the spot?
(Both of them hide.)
(Kalapahad's soldiers flee. Odia soldiers pursue. Banambar and Sadashib come out of the hiding.)

BANA : Oh, saved! Are you breathing freely, brother, Sadashib? I am panting for

		breath. Oh, My God! Fighting. I was not coming. You forced me to come.
SADA	:	They are very well running away speedily! Are you afraid, Banambar? No, there is no need to panic.
BANA	:	Afraid? No, never. Had there been a fight in the king's palace, they would have run away like this. But there was not much space there. They should have gone to a field.
SADA	:	One would have chased and the other would have fled. Our king would have chased or fled. It's not bad that Kalapahad had caught hold of him. He should have run helter-skelter. He is now without worries. Well, tell me, "Who will win?"
BANA	:	Kalapahad will win. These are after them from now. Is it not clear? One side must win. The other will be defeated. If two parties win, it is difficult to tell, 'Who won?' and 'Who lost? How can the winner be decided if both the parties win, or both lose? They might be drawing lots.

(*There is too much noise and sounds of clashing weapons from the background.*)
Again. Again. They are fast approaching. In which way shall we flee?
(Muslim *Soldiers enter.*)

SADA	:	Which way?
SOLDIER	:	Are you the same person who escaped from us in the fort of Ramachandra Bhanja?
SADASHIV	:	No. I am not.

MUKUNDA DEB | 133

2nd SOLDIER	:	Yes, he is. (*Kills Sadashib with his sword.*)
BANA	:	Oh, how much blood! Don't kill me. Don't kill me. (*Exit.*)

(*On orders from Kalapahad, Muslim soldiers turn back and the battle ensues. The Army Chief is killed. Raghunath is severely injured. Muslim soldiers again run away. Minister and the remaining Odia soldiers chase them.*)

RAGHU : (*tries to get up and collapses.*) What a blow! The Chief is killed. There is no more time left for me, Minister. It is hopeless. Nothing more. Comprehensive defeat! What a bleak future! The state is in ruins. Oh, how painful! What a suffering! Good bye, Motherland. How lusterless you look! Tears are flowing down like the flow of water in the Mahanadi. Who will wipe them? Shall I try to get up once more? (*tries to get up and collapses.*) No, it's not possible. I am dying. Oh, soldiers, you are strewn everywhere, rolling in the dust. No. No more. Good bye!

(*Curtain*)

SCENE III
The Yard outside Leelabati's Room.

(*Leelabati enter.*)

LEELA : Am I alive? Very well alive. Why should I live any longer? For how many days? For whom? Everything is finished now. The sun has once risen in my life due to my good luck. It is already set now. My

		dearest is imprisoned by the enemies, tortured, and at death's door. My dearest! I couldn't save you. I am a sinner. I am a sinner, Ushayinee. I am being punished for it. The kingdom is in ruins. Everything is finished. Why should I continue to live? Are you returning, dearest? Are you alive? Will you try? Who is left? Raghunath is no more. Banambar! He is my last hope! Is it my punishment? Expiation for my sin? Is there any hope? I am a sinner. I shall go. Will you come back, dearest? Shall I take leave of you? (*Handmaid enters.*) Sulakshana!
MAID	:	Kalapahad is telling to release Maharaj.
LEELA	:	Why, Sulakshana?
MAID	:	He says that it is no longer required.
LEELA	:	Will Maharaj come back? No, it is impossible, Sulakshana. Only once. My days are numbered. Only once, I like to say, 'I am leaving.' I'll take leave of him. I'll mingle myself with five elements. All enjoyments are over. The rest is that I shall end my life. Is it possible. Do you say that it is possible? Who knows? Take me with you, Sulakshana. Take me. I am unable to stand up.
MAID	:	(*holding Leelabati.*) Let's go, your Highness. (*Curtain*)

SCENE IV
The Field Outside Kalapahad's Camp.
(*Kalapahad is standing.*)

KALA : I have won this state. I have occupied the jeweled throne of Utkal. I can be an emperor if I like. No. that is not my goal. To govern a kingdom is not my duty now. Victory and power – they are enough for me. Now I'll preach my religion with the help of my sword as Prophet Mohammad had done. Still there is one more task left. Barabati. Without it my victory is incomplete. The queen is in possession of it. What a stupid Queen! It is not a bad proposal. It is a nice metamorphosis from the vanquished to a victor. Why is there an objection to it? She will be a beggar in the streets. A woman with her tender arms is trying to keep up the sovereignty of the country in which the King and the Chief of the Army are defeated by this powerful force. What stupidity! These arms are fit to embrace the paramour in love, Queen. I told you that though old but with the aroma of butter you would incline to the new emperor as the delightful Queen. It did not matter with you. You turned me down. You kicked my offer. Kicks from the vanquished! This is severe humiliation for the Muslim blood. You would have been the precious jewel in my life. Now you are my enemy. We would have engaged

	yourself in the battle of love. But there will now be meeting of the sharp blades of our swords. Well, I'll see. *(Banambar enters.)* Who's there?
BANA	: I have come from Sarang Garh. The Queen has sent me.
KALA	: Why?
BANA	: You are now the emperor, so this is a customary visit.
KALA	: You can meet me in the streets outside the camp. This is not our custom.
BANA	: The queen has a proposal for you. She has sent some gifts.
KALA	: Proposal! No, I shall not listen to any proposal. I don't believe in the women of this kingdom. Your Queen should understand that I'm not here to be governed by a frail woman. Yet I will listen to you. Then, citizen, what is the proposal?
BANA	: If you release the king, she will attend on him. She has given this gift for you.
KALA	: Keep the gift with you. We will set the king free. Who is there? *(Voice from the background : Your Majesty!)*
KALA	: You will take the king with you. *(Guard enters.)* Look, Guard. Bring the king of Saranga Garh here.
GUARD	: The servant of Allah! Your Majesty! *(Exit.)*
KALA	: Tell your Queen that I am very much

MUKUNDA DEB | 137

pleased with her conduct. It's not a bad proposal from the Queen. It's not a proposal of the Queen, not a prayer but her command. This command is very sweet. Tell the Queen that she might sometimes command me like this.
(*Guard enters along with Ramachandra Bhanja.*)
Here comes the King!

RAMA : Look, Dhurjati, Narasingha will be the king. Shall I tolerate this? Go, Dhurjati, go. Finish him with this sword. Is the task finished, Dhurjati? Very fine. The story of Narasingha took place one year ago. Again Raghurama. No, it mustn't be. Confidential! Very confidential! You will go to hell, Raghurama. Couldn't you do it, Dhurjati? Mukunda will come to your house, to your sword. All ruined, Dhurjati. Couldn't you do it? He is a demon, the old Dhanurdhar. Did you leave him too? War. Now war. The throne of Odisha! If I'm destined! But the minister. He can't be trusted. No, Dhurjati, finish him first. Oh, good riddance! Shikhi and Manai, tell Kalapahad that half the state is his. Can Mukunda be able to? But, Dhurjati, you are a killer. Will you come? No, go away. Go by that way. How relieved I am now! Oh, pure gold, King! Oh!

KALA : Is there anything more?
RAMA : Stay close to Mukunda Deb. Is it done properly, Manai? You could not.

	Dependence on others! No, stupid Queen, off with you. Truce! Truce! Go, Mukunda. There is no hurdle on my way now. But Kalapahad! I'll take care. Here is Dhanurdhar! With one blow, Sadashib. Imprisonment! Imprisonment! No, no, only for once! Don't imprison me, Kalapahad. No. No. No. (*runs away.*)
KALA	: Watch out!
	(B*anambar and guard exit.*)
	Atonement is as good as sin. There is no peace in life. There is no need for food and sleep. First Barabati. Let me check. Stupid Queen, your place will be occupied by the Queen of Sarang Garh.
	(*Curtain*)

SCENE V
A burning fire at Barabati.

(*Ushayinee and other women of the city are standing.*)

USHA	: Here is noise of victory. Are you ready? Have let your hair loose? Have you been properly dressed? There is no time for delay. We protected this fort for two months. Our tender arms could put up with the attack of the sharp Muslim weapons. We drenched the walls of the fort with Muslim blood. We filled the ground beside the fort with Muslim corpses. It's impossible now. The Muslims are thrilled for their victory. Come, the women of the city. Let's finish the job. The fire is

burning fiercely. (*shouts of victory*) Why is this scream? How excited the enemy is! Let's not delay. Listen. What screams! (*Again, shouts of victory*) Did the Muslims pull down the fort wall? Why this loud screaming? Let's not delay. They might enter before long. Now they did. Come, let's mingle these tiny flames of our lives with the gigantic fire in the pyre. Come, women. Come, Bhadra, Jayanti, Manjari, Sweta, and Bilashini. Come, all of you. The fire is burning quite brilliantly.

1st WOMAN : (Song)
Oh, fire, burn, more fiercely burn,
Let the golden flames into the sky rise.
Quickly burn these wretched women,
In accepting our final prayers. (*enters the pyre.*)
2nd WOMAN : (Song)
We have finished our womanly chores,
Leaving our souls with the hubbies,
Bringing an end to all desires
Burn us, oh, holy fires! (*enters the pyre.*)
3rd WOMAN : (Song)
Oh, my dear! You closed his eyes in the war,
What is the need of this life,
As I couldn't save the fort, dear? (*enters the pyre.*)
(*Chitrotpala enters.*)

CHITRO	:	Will you jump into the fire, Mother?
USHA	:	Yes, I will. Oh, Chitra, the apple of my eye!
CHITRO	:	Please, loosen my hair, mother. I'll jump into the fire.
USHA	:	Will you? Were you born to burn yourself?
CHITRO	:	Why are you crying, mother?

USHA	:	Dear Chitra, I will pity for you. No. No.
CHITRO	:	Are you still crying? Aren't we jumping into fire? Why don't you say anything?
USHA	:	Yes, we will, dear.
CHITRO	:	Shall we be burnt up, or shall we be still living like this?
USHA	:	Dear Chitra, stay here. I'm going first.
CHITRO	:	No, mother. I'll jump first.
USHA	:	No, Chitra. I tell you. Why don't you obey me?
CHITRO	:	I do. I'll jump first. Shall I be burnt up if I jump into fire like them?
USHA	:	Yes, you will, dear.
CHITRO	:	My cascade of hair will be burnt up, won't they?
USHA	:	Yes, dear. You make me sentimental, Chitra. No, I should not delay.
CHITRO	:	My eyes?
USHA	:	They will.
CHITRO	:	Then, how can I see, mother?
USHA	:	Wait, dear. Let me enter the fire first. Then, you will. Wait, I am going. (*attempts to enter the pyre.*)
CHITRO	:	Wait, mother. What will happen if I am burnt up?
USHA	:	Ah! My dear Chitrotpala. My destiny was used up. Only you were left. Now you will be finished. What didn't you do, oh, my God? (*screams of victory from the background.*) My turn has come, Chitra. I am late, dear. I am going. (*Both of them approach fire.*) (*Leelabati enters.*)

LEELA	:	Ushayini! (*Chitrotpala enters fire. Ushayinee turns back.*)
USHA	:	Who? Did you go, Chitra dear? Whose voice is it? Leelabati? How are you here at this hour, sister?
LEELA	:	This is the last act of life. I'll bring an end to it here, Ushayinee. I have bid farewell to all for good. There is nothing left in this life, sister. Only my husband is left. I have nursed him, done wifely duties, nursed him back to health. I have taken his permission, bid him farewell. There is no place left for me neither on this earth nor in water nor in the skies. I'll finish myself here.
USHA	:	No, sister, this is a blunder. Husband is the half of wife's life. You have no right to bid farewell to him. Both husband and wife are each other's companion either in happiness or in sorrow, either in heaven or in hell, either in life or in death. This is selfishness; a temptation for the luxury of happiness. You have made a great mistake, sister. You have to live in perpetual happiness or sorrow, prosperity and adversity together as long as the husband is with you. We are the daughters of Mother Utkal, Leelabati. We are like tender flowers for the husband and son. How can we be so rough? No, go back, sister, go back.
LEELA	:	As you are telling me, I shall go back, Ushayinee. I am a puppet of wood now. I have no knowledge of good or bad.

		(*screams of victory from the background.*) What is this noise?
USHA	:	Don't delay, sister. Go back. How will you go? How did you come?
LEELA	:	By a secret path. My old maid showed me the way.
USHA	:	What about Muslims?
LEELA	:	No one was there.
USHA	:	No, Muslims have assembled at the gate of the fort. They are overwhelmed with the joy of victory. Never delay. Go back by that way, sister. Go, hurry up.
LEELA	:	This is our last meeting, Ushayinee. Shall I go. Bye. (*shouts of victory from the background.*)
USHA	:	Go, sister Leelabati. Don't delay. (*bids farewell to Leelabati.*) Good bye. You are the last flash of lightning in the cruel expansive firmament of the fort. All is quiet here now. How horrible aloneness is! Dear Chitra, are you burnt up? No one is here so that I can have a glimpse. All attachments and affections are severed! This lovely fort is now an impassable desert, silent, still and lonely. Only the screams of victorious Muslims outside the fort wall are disturbing the terrible silence. (*shouts of victory from the background.*) Good sound! Nice shouts of victory! The dearest Lord of my life is on the opposite side of the pyre. Please take into your refuge, dear. (*shouts of victory from the background.*) The shouts of victory are rising higher

and higher. Who is this? This, of course, is not Leelabati. Oh, Musalman! The last weapon of a woman has been consigned to fire, the fire which burnt up my dear Chitra. Well, Come Musalman! Though a frail woman, I shall rest in fire after trying the strength of my arms on your victorious head. How can I leave the fort as long as I survive? That can never be. Till now the fort belongs to the women of the city. How radiant the Muslim is! How he runs in victorious arrogance!
(*Kalapahad enters.*)

KALA : Even now dear, I shall give you shelter in my arms.

USHA : Be off, Muslim. (*kicks him.*)

KALA : (*trembling*) Again that kick. Well, there is no respite, woman. (*raises his sword.*)
(*Ushayinee is wounded but kicks Kalapahad so hard that he is flung afar. He tries to rise.*)

USHA : Please, accept me, mother. (*enters the pyre.*)
(*Curtain*)

Black Eagle Books

www.blackeaglebooks.org
info@blackeaglebooks.org

Black Eagle Books, an independent publisher, was founded as a nonprofit organization in April, 2019. It is our mission to connect and engage the Indian diaspora and the world at large with the best of works of world literature published on a collaborative platform, with special emphasis on foregrounding Contemporary Classics and New Writing.

www.ingramcontent.com/pod-product-compliance
Lightning Source LLC
Chambersburg PA
CBHW060611080526
44585CB00013B/783